Teaching Challenges
in Secondary Schools

Teaching Challenges in Secondary Schools

Cases in Educational Psychology

Alyssa R. Gonzalez-DeHass and
Patricia P. Willems

ROWMAN & LITTLEFIELD
Lanham • Boulder • New York • London

Published by Rowman & Littlefield
A wholly owned subsidiary of The Rowman & Littlefield Publishing Group, Inc.
4501 Forbes Boulevard, Suite 200, Lanham, Maryland 20706
www.rowman.com

Unit A, Whitacre Mews, 26-34 Stannary Street, London SE11 4AB

British Library Cataloguing in Publication Information Available

Library of Congress Cataloging-in-Publication Data is Available

ISBN 978-1-4758-2818-4 (cloth: alk. paper)
ISBN 978-1-4758-2819-1 (pbk: alk. paper)
ISBN 978-1-4758-2820-7 (electronic)

♾™ The paper used in this publication meets the minimum requirements of American National Standard for Information Sciences—Permanence of Paper for Printed Library Materials, ANSI/NISO Z39.48-1992.

Printed in the United States of America

Dear Ava, Maddox, Logan, Emma, and Gavin: May your classrooms be places of discovery, exploration, and inspiration. May your teachers ignite your imagination and instill a love of learning so that you are able to appreciate your unique potential, persevere in your learning, and realize your dreams.

Dear Future Teacher: Adolescence is a time of growing independence and expanding opportunities. Encourage students to embrace their strengths and seek out meaningful occasions to extend their learning.

Contents

Introduction

WHY CASE INSTRUCTION?

Case studies present real-life classroom scenarios that reflect the challenges actual classroom teachers experience in today's secondary classrooms. Utilizing case studies is particularly vital for educational psychology courses that do not require a field component where students would have a chance to apply information firsthand in the schools. Case study learning experiences are the next best thing to actual classroom opportunities, and they may even be an important first step. They provide students the chance to see the relevance of educational psychology material and afford them an opportunity to practice hypothetical teacher decision making.

The cases in this text depict key challenges that teachers face in today's middle and high schools: academic honesty and Internet plagiarism, complaining and arguing about grades, back talk and disrespect, cyberbullying, adolescent cliques, academic pressures of high school, encouraging female students in STEM learning, the power of social media, cell phones in the classroom, encounters with difficult parents, and finding and grading meaningful alternative assessment options. However, these classroom dilemmas are embedded within the domains of learning common across coursework in educational psychology: human development, individual differences, learning theories, motivation, classroom management, instruction, and assessment practices.

Engaging in discussion and decision making about critical classroom challenges may have enormous benefits for preservice teachers' learning, and these include gaining an appreciation for the realities of classroom teaching, opportunities for authentic learning experiences, scaffolding of critical thinking skills, and becoming engaged and motivated in learning about educational psychology (Gonzalez-DeHass & Willems, 2015). Because of their narrative nature, cases engage students' interest and capture their attention (Ching, 2011). Further, case instruction may assist preservice teachers in bridging theory and practice (Engle & Faux, 2006; Patrick, Anderman, Bruening, & Duffin, 2011), promote students' capacity to apply psychological constructs and their critical analysis of educational situations (Bruning et al., 2008; PytilikZillig et al., 2011), and encourage students' intrinsic motivation for learning (DeMarco, Hayward, & Lynch, 2002; Mayo, 2002).

TO GET THE MOST OUT OF CASE INSTRUCTION

This case study book presents coverage of all of the main topical areas in educational psychology and provides open-ended questions targeting the specific theories. Instructors can use these questions as discussion or incorporate them into assignments. Identified key practices in case study instruction may be particularly helpful for students' learning: establishing a collaborative community of learners, encouraging perspective taking of various stakeholders in a case, scaffolding students' reflection and critical-thinking skills during case analyses, revisiting cases using different theoretical viewpoints or at different points in the course, and transitioning class discussions into a culminating writing assignment (Gonzalez-DeHass & Willems, 2015).

The cases in this text have been developed with these tips in mind, and they are centered around teaching challenges that middle and high school teachers are facing in today's classrooms. Case study instruction should encourage students to consider classroom solutions from the viewpoint of different classroom stakeholders (Heitzmann, 2008; Sudzina, 1997). Some of the cases are written from the student's perspective while others may be from the teacher's standpoint, and we encourage you to examine the challenges in the case from multiple stakeholders' viewpoints. For example, case 9, *Grade Grubbing: Complaining and Arguing about Grades*, allows the reader to consider the viewpoint of the teacher and student. The student is having trouble employing successful learning strategies to do well in class, and the teacher struggles with how to respond effectively when a student consistently makes excuses and complains about her grades. The most effective resolution will consider both perspectives surrounding this challenge.

Another suggestion for effective case instruction involves instructor and students revisiting cases at a later point in their course. During initial discussions, students become versed in the language of individual theories and their application to authentic classroom challenges, but as they gain more experience with case analysis they become more reflective, more cognizant of effective practices, and less likely to resort to the simplest answer (Sudzina,

1997). For example, case 7, *Cell Phones in Class: Problems with Texting*, can be first introduced in an adolescent development lesson to discuss peer relationships and the impact of social media at these ages. However, the instructor could return to the case later in the course when covering topics on classroom management and how cell phones in the classroom can disrupt instruction. Sometimes this discussion will take place within small-group work as students' brainstorm solutions to teaching challenges before joining in whole-class discussion. Regardless of group format, when students are encouraged to talk about classroom teaching practices it cultivates a collaborative learning environment that engages them in decision making under the guidance of their course instructor.

STANDARDS AND PRINCIPLES

The cases featured in this book can be easily linked to the Learner-Centered Psychological Principles published by the American Psychological Association (APA) (Learner-Centered Principles Work Group of the American Psychological Association's Board of Educational Affairs, 1997) and the model core teaching standards of the Interstate Teacher Assessment and Support Consortium (INTASC) (Council of Chief State School Officers, 2011). We chose to include these principles and standards due to their relevance to the field of educational psychology and their commitment to improving education. The APA Learner-Centered Psychological Principles offer a useful structure for improving schools by integrating improved teaching practices centered on the learner and aimed at the active learning process. There are fourteen APA learner-centered psychological principles under four factors: cognitive and metacognitive factors, motivational and affective factors, developmental and social factors, and individual differences factors. Each factor includes a set of principles that relate to that factor as well as an in-depth description of each principle (the full document may be viewed at https://www.apa.org/ed/governance/bea/learner-centered.pdf).

The INTASC Model Core Teaching Standards describe essential effective teaching ideologies for the sole purpose of improving student success. These standards are applicable across all grades and school subjects and are relevant to the field of educational psychology. There are ten INTASC Model Core Teaching Standards that are divided into four categories: the learner and learning, content knowledge, instructional practice, and professional responsibility. In general, the INTASC Model Core Teaching Standards emphasize the importance of student-centered instructional methods that appreciate individual differences between learners and where students apply the knowledge

they learn to the real world (the full document can be viewed at http://
www.ccsso.org/Resources/Publications/InTASC_Model_Core_Teaching_
Standards_and_Learning_Progressions_for_Teachers_10.html).

Standards and Principles: Linking to the Cases

The themes outlined in both the INTASC Model Core Teaching Standards and
the APA Learner-Centered Psychological Principles provide a framework for
applying the educational psychology theories that the case studies in this book
are centered on. The link between the standards and principles and the theories found in the cases allows students and instructors to make connections
between standards in the field for effective teaching practices and theoretical knowledge. For example, the second factor in the APA learner-centered
psychological principles is motivational and affective factors, which house
motivational and emotional influences on learning and intrinsic motivation
to learn. These two learner-centered psychological principles tie to part V of
the casebook, which introduces the motivation section and contains cases 10
and 11, that introduce various aspects of motivation such as goal orientations,
attributions, self-efficacy, and self-regulation.

Similarly, the educational psychology concepts and theories addressed
in the cases are able to be associated to the INTASC Model Core Teaching
Standards. For instance, the first category of the INTASC Model Core Teaching Standards focuses on the learner and learning, and it contains three standards: learner development, learning differences, and learning environments.
This category's first standard on learner development ties to the development
section of the casebook comprised of cases 1–4. The first four cases of the
book all deal with numerous aspects of human development, and the cases'
suggested theories include various developmental concepts such as cognitive,
social, psychosocial, and moral development. They focus on those issues
most pertinent to adolescent development. The second standard under this
category is learning differences, and it can be linked to part II of the casebook
on individual differences and diversity, which is comprised of cases 5 and 6.
These case studies' topics range from a variety of aspects of learner differences including gender roles and exceptional student education. Finally, the
third standard in this category is learning environments, which relates to the
third part of the casebook, learning theories, composed of cases 7–9. These
cases have themes that cover various aspects relating directly to creating a
productive student learning environment such as the use of classical conditioning, applications of social cognitive theory, and information processing.
In addition, even though certain units will have a more emphasized role for
each theory, some theories will nevertheless weave throughout different parts
of the book given the complex dynamics evident in today's classrooms.

In addition, a second book, *Case Studies in Educational Psychology: Elementary School Grades*, presents cases that raise issues important for teaching challenges most evident for teachers in the elementary school grades. This allows preservice teachers interested in teaching younger students a chance to engage in hypothetical decision making for issues that elementary teachers face today. These include challenges surrounding kindergarten readiness, teaching respect and kindness, teasing, disruptive and defiant behavior, cheating, handling student excuses, teaching gifted and culturally diverse learners, preparing twenty-first-century learners, mindful use of technology in the classroom, and balancing instructional time with state testing requirements.

REFERENCES

Bruning, R., Siwatu, K. O., Liu, X., PytlikZillig, L. M., Horn, C., Sic, S., & Carslon, D. (2008). Introducing teaching cases with face-to-face and computer-mediated discussion: Two multi-classroom quasi-experiments. *Contemporary Educational Psychology, 33*, 299–326.

Ching, C. P. (2011). Preservice teachers' use of educational theories in classroom and behavior management course: A case based approach. *Procedia: Social and Behavioral Sciences, 29*, 1209–1217.

Council of Chief State School Officers. (2011, April). *Interstate teacher assessment and support consortium (InTASC) model core teaching standards: A resource for state dialogue.* Washington, DC: CC550. Retrieved February 20, 2017, from http://www.ccsso.org/documents/2011/intasc_model_core_teaching_standards_2011.pdf

DeMarco, R., Hayward, L., & Lynch, M. (2002). Nursing students' experiences with strategic approaches to case-based instruction: A replication and comparison study between two disciplines. *Journal of Nursing Education, 41*(4), 165–174.

Engle, R. A., & Faux, R. B. (2006). Towards productive disciplinary engagement of prospective teachers in educational psychology: Comparing two methods of case-based instruction. *Teaching Educational Psychology, 1*(2), 1–22.

Heitzmann, R. (2008). Case study instruction in teacher education: Opportunity to develop students' critical thinking, school smarts and decision-making. *Education, 128*(4), 523–542.

Gonzalez-DeHass, A. R., & Willems, P. P. (2015). Case study instruction in educational psychology: Implications for teacher preparation. In M. Li & Y. Zhao (Eds.), *Exploring Learning and Teaching in Higher Education.* New York: Springer.

Learner-Centered Principles Work Group of the American Psychological Association's Board of Educational Affairs. (1997, November). *Learner-centered psychological principles: A framework for school redesign.* Retrieved February 20, 2017, from https://www.apa.org/ed/governance/bea/learner-centered.pdf

Mayo, J. A. (2002). Case-based instruction: A technique for increasing conceptual application in introductory psychology. *Journal of Constructivist Psychology, 15*, 65–74.

Patrick, H., Anderman, L. H., Bruening, P. S., & Duffin, L. C. (2011). The role of educational psychology in teacher education: Three challenges for educational psychologists. *Educational Psychologist, 46*(2), 71–83.

PytlikZillig, L. M., Horn, C. A., Bruning, R., Bell, S., Liu, X., Siwatu, K. O., Bodvarsson, M. C., Doyoung, K., & Carlson, D. (2011). Face-to-face versus computer-mediated discussion of teaching cases: Impacts on preservice teachers' engagement, critical analyses, and self-efficacy. *Contemporary Educational Psychology, 36*, 302–312.

Sudzina, M. R. (1997). Case study as a constructivist pedagogy for teaching educational psychology. *Educational Psychology Review, 9*(2), 199–218.

Part I

HUMAN DEVELOPMENT

Case 1

Adolescent Cliques

To Belong or Not to Belong?

Suggested Theories/Content: Adolescent Development, Erikson's Theory of Personality Development and Identity, Observational Learning, Peer Modeling, Cooperative Learning, and Parent Involvement
Teacher Challenges: Bullying, Peer-Acceptance, Social Media, Social Well-Being
Student Level: High School

Mike Turner is a ninth-grade teacher with a few years of teaching experience under his belt. He is a well-liked faculty member at the school, and he is known for establishing excellent rapport with students. He teaches English literature and is known for his innovation and dedication. Frequently, he is seen hauling props to complement his instruction of the latest reading assignment. Many teachers respect his enthusiasm and his talent for engaging otherwise recalcitrant students.

It is the third week of school and Mr. Turner is waiting for his fourth-period literature class to make their way into the classroom; this class period is always a bit slower trickling in since many students are returning from their lunch periods. As Mr. Turner prepares for the upcoming assignment he notices Gina Simmons making her way into the classroom. Gina is known as being different since she dresses in dark colors and has noticeably dyed black hair, and the only makeup she wears is a very dark smattering of black eyeliner.

He secretly smiles at her choice of outfit today; she tends to favor T-shirts that have popular sayings or that poke fun at pop culture. While her apparel does not break the school dress code because it is not offensive in nature, her attire does certainly offer an insight into this student's viewpoint. Gina is one of Mr. Turner's best students who always completes her homework assignments and has much to offer in class discussions.

Before he gets further in his musings, he notices that one of the more tightly knit group of girls, a student named Lila in particular, is observing Gina's entrance. The clique immediately begins to whisper and engage in obvious snickering at Gina. Mr. Turner knows that this group of girls has had similar reactions to Gina before, and therefore he takes that opportunity to walk by Lila's desk and predictably, the girls cease their discussion.

Mr. Turner passes out the week's upcoming assignment on Shakespeare, and the students begin work independently. He sees that as Gina begins working on the assignment, she looks over where Lila is sitting with her clique, and it's clear that they are making fun of her again. He remembers Gina saying that there was a time when she and Lila were best friends and spent all their time together.

Then, last summer, she said it all changed because Lila met a new group of friends while attending cheerleading camp, and instantly they formed a tight clique. Lila stopped returning Gina's texts and declined all her invitations to get together. Gina could see on Lila's social media accounts that with each passing day Lila was not only well established with her new friends but that she was clearly their leader. Gina alluded to him that she and Lila had drifted apart; then once school started Lila's clique was actively going out of their way to upset her.

A few days later Mr. Turner is concluding a class discussion on Hamlet. The class is just finishing a discussion of the interaction between Hamlet and Ophelia that occurs in the third act when Gina begins to offer a comment. "Well, you know, Mr. Turner, I read that act very carefully because . . ." Lila sarcastically interrupts, "Really? I'm surprised! You had time to read the assigned pages? Shocking! Don't you spend all of your time with your weird group of friends? Whatever you call yourselves these days . . . talking about music, drinking, chatting up where the next party is going to be."

The looks of condescension and dislike coming from Lila's friends are an obvious show of support for Lila's offensive. Gina noticeably tenses, but her facial expression barely changes when she replies, "How would you know what we talk about? You are too scared to step out of your small little world to even listen to what other people might be interested in just because they look a little different than you." Mr. Turner watches as the rest of the class observes with noticeable interest whether there will be any forthcoming invectives from Lila's crew.

However, Mr. Turner fears that this can escalate quickly and decides to redirect the class by reminding everyone of the merits of a sense of camaraderie in their shared learning endeavor in his classroom. He also reiterates in a firm manner that they all know that he adamantly discourages any instances of disrespectful comments during class discussions. He makes sure to say this with a pointed look at Lila and the rest of the girls in the clique. He then quickly moves forward in the lesson making a mental note to look a bit deeper into this issue and arrange the seating chart so that Lila and her group are separated.

At end of the week, Mr. Turner is grading the students' writing assignment on Hamlet. Mr. Turner is looking over the typical distribution of grades, and noticing those students who always seem to have trouble, are still having trouble. He is reflecting on some way to reach these students, but the truth is he is not sure where the problem lies. Are they truly having trouble grasping the subtleties of English literature, or are they not finishing the reading?

As he is reflecting on possible instructional strategies available to him, he also factors in the ongoing tension between Gina and Lila's camp. And as much as Gina seems to do well with the subtleties of Shakespearean literature, more and more she disengages from classroom discussion just to avoid confrontations with Lila, which she knows that the whole class will be audience to. Clearly, the other students in the class are not willing to stand up to Lila and her friends, and the result is that Gina is rather ostracized.

Gina also seems to be having confrontations with some of the other girls in the clique. Just yesterday, there was another altercation between Gina and Sharon, one of the other members of Lila's clique, at the end of class. Gina made a derogatory comment about Sharon's obsession with the "hottest" boy in school—Justin Drake. Justin is a very popular athlete whom many girls like; however, Gina commented on how much Sharon shares about her liking Justin on social media and that Justin would never like her.

"Gina, do you really think that because he allowed you to tutor him so he can keep his grades up that means you two are friends?" Sharon had asked, seemingly appalled before continuing, "Get real! He only lowered himself to talk to you because he had to! The tutor program is there to help the athletes and you were assigned to him! I bet he doesn't even know your name . . . just knows you as the creepy, bizarre girl tutor that the coach assigned to him." Lila and the rest of the girls had all quickly agreed, and again, while the rest of the students in the class watched the exchange, they did not intervene.

Obviously, the line of demarcation displayed here runs deeper than his typical approach to distract with the wonders literature has to offer. And, technically, the hostilities are always just inside of the rules of the classroom, so he really doesn't have a classroom management issue so much as an atmosphere of dislike that is beginning to distract the class and is certainly creating a negative learning atmosphere. He decides to take the issue home and mull it over a bit more.

Later that day, Mike is walking down the main hallway to the faculty parking lot when he encounters one of his colleagues, Ned Reilly. After the typical banter associated with the end of a school day, Mike fills him in on the situation between the girls and his concerns over Gina's sense of academic comfort in his classroom.

As they reach the door that goes out to the parking lot, Ned pauses, but Mike observes that Ned doesn't seem surprised. In fact, Mike learns that Ned is quite familiar with Lila and her clique. Ned says, "Don't forget, Mike, you've got them right at the beginning of their high school transition. This is a tricky time for them. You see, I have Lila in my second-period geometry course. And in my class, Lila sharpens her claws on one of my other female students who is a bit overweight.

"These students are confronted with puberty and body image issues and an interest in the opposite sex all at the same time. Many of these popular kids are used to being the 'top dog' of the middle school, and now they are the lowest 'rung of the ladder,' so to speak, with the older high school grades. So they have to prove their worth and establish their place within the popular crowds, which unfortunately with Lila's group, means outwardly picking on girls that are seen as different. And, as they all try to figure out who they are and where they fit in, at the same time that they are trying to distance themselves from their parents.

"Then you throw in the effect of social media, which doesn't help this situation in the least; if anything it inflames it. It is no wonder that these tensions arise." Mike sets his briefcase down for a moment and takes a deep breath while Ned continues. "It is no wonder that their motivations lie elsewhere! You are trying to engage them in thoughtful discussions of Hamlet's plight, and there are obviously numerous sources competing with you for their attention. Like who posted what on their social media accounts, who went where and with whom, who is dating whom, who is having a party! And as you are witnessing, who doesn't like whom." Mike nods in agreement.

"So you think these girls' parents are aware of all that is happening between them at school? I heard from one of my students that Lila and Gina were close friends and that their parents socialized together, so they must know, right?" Mike asks with a measure of hope.

"Well, that depends. Many parents do not know what their teenagers are up to online, and they do not regularly monitor their high schoolers' social media presence. Hence, they are not likely to be aware of all that is truly happening in their lives. Even if these parents are friendly with each other, they might just assume that their daughters grew apart due to different interests—Lila is now a popular cheerleader involved in all school events and sports and dating and socializing with jocks. Her parents might see her separation from Gina as a natural transition for Lila and not that she is being malicious and intentionally snubbing Gina," Ned says honestly.

"Yes, unfortunately, I see your point. Students at this age are fighting to establish their independence and their identity, and parents may feel that they are helping them by giving them more leeway in their social pursuits as well as respecting their privacy on social media," Mike responds as the men wave to other colleagues walking to their cars.

"Exactly, and remember too, it's difficult for working parents with multiple children to keep up with all of the social media avenues that are available out there to teens. It can seem overwhelming to parents. Some feel that navigating social relationships is all a part of the adolescent world, and they may assume that as long as their kids don't come to them for assistance, they are doing fine."

Mike reflects a minute before offering, "You know, perhaps I need to continue to focus my efforts in the classroom then. I had already been considering the idea of cooperative learning to cure another problem I have been experiencing. I have about a handful of students who just are not doing well in my class. So, I had been thinking about establishing heterogeneous group learning exercises to allow for some peer scaffolding. Given the research literature on cooperative learning pointing to positive social outcomes, attitudes, and social skills, maybe I can help to alleviate two ills at the same time. Maybe if I can get them involved in a common cause they will be able to relate better with each other, especially if I break up Lila's group, which I had already thought to do, and scatter those students who are struggling with the academic concepts into groups with other students who have had stellar performance so far."

Ned smiles and adds, "You know I was reading an article that discussed the benefits of cooperative learning activities. In addition to listing cooperative learning's benefits in the classroom it also addressed the importance of involving parents and community leaders in the school. This is certainly something that you can bring up at the next department meeting since it is speaking to a school-wide effort. I mean you are the one with the great rep who could pioneer this effort," Ned says mischievously, clearly amused with his witty comment as he pats Mike on the back.

"Ha! You aren't really suggesting that I alone tackle all the problems of high school teaching. And whatever happened to collegiality?" Mike asks, laughing at his friend's gibe. "How about we both agree to discuss this idea at the next meeting; the administration is always looking for innovative ways to establish home-school partnerships," Mike says amused. Both men laugh as they say their goodbyes and get into their cars.

DISCUSSION QUESTIONS

1. Developmental Issues of Adolescence
   a. According to Piaget, identify the stage of cognitive development students are likely to be in. How is that likely to play a role in their behavior?

b. Explain how Elkind's adolescent egocentrism could be of significance when understanding the reasons for their actions? Discuss ways that teachers can assist students in reducing their adolescent egocentrism.
c. Discuss the role that social media plays in an adolescents' cognitive development? How may it impede, rather than assist, adolescents' cognitive growth?

2. Socioemotional Development
   a. Explain how peers play a role in this case. What effects do cliques have on an adolescents' behavior?
   b. Speculate how adolescent friendships and their social well-being in general can be affected by a student's involvement in social media.
   c. How can Gina's self-esteem and self-concept be affected by the opposing clique's actions?
   d. Discuss how you could apply Bronfenbrenner's Ecological Systems theory to this case. Which of Bronfenbrenner's Ecological Systems would be most influential in this case?
   e. Anticipate how teachers might respond to student cliques and the inevitable consequence of some students feeling left out.
   f. Discuss the dangers of bullying. What role does social media play in enabling bullying and cyberbullying?
   g. What signs should teachers look for to help identify students who are being bullied? What differences exist with regard to gender and bullying? Discuss physical versus relational aggression.
   h. How can schools implement school-wide programs to increase the awareness of bullying and to prevent and stop bullying?

3. Erikson's Theory of Personality Development and Identity
   a. Discuss which stage of Erikson's theory these students are likely to be in. How are the events of the case affecting students' development of identity?
   b. How might teachers' awareness of Erikson's theory impact their classroom teacher decision making?
   c. How can teachers assist their students' development of identity? What examples of this were evident in the case?
   d. Explain, from Marcia's identity development, where each of the main characters are with respect to their identity status. How is that evident in the case?
   e. Discuss how each of Marcia's identity statuses might help to describe how a person's identity forms.

4. Observational Learning and Peer Modeling
   a. What role might observational learning play in students' clique-like behavior?
   b. What role does social reinforcement play in clique-like behavior? What is a dominance hierarchy within a clique? How does the use of sarcasm and ridicule reinforce group boundaries?
   c. What role does television and the film industry play in the potential for broader social modeling to explain adolescent cliques? How can teachers expose students to positive symbolic models?
   d. In what ways can teachers be a positive influence and role model of tolerance?
   e. Discuss cooperative learning's benefits for helping students appreciate individual differences as well as expose students to peer modeling of academic skills. Why is heterogeneous grouping so important?
   f. How would the teacher ensure both individual accountability and an incentive to cooperate among students during small-group work?

5. Parent Involvement
   a. How can teachers increase parent involvement at the high school level?
   b. Explain why teachers tend to see a drop in parent involvement at the high school level.
   c. Decide on ways in which parents might realistically be involved in the high schools that would be comfortable for both parents and students? In particular, in what ways might parents serve as coaches or mentors to adolescents?
   d. Identify specific ways to facilitate home-school communication. Develop a list of tips for effective parent-teacher conferencing with parents of older high school students.

Case 2

Internet Plagiarism

Suggested Theories: Cognitive Development in Adolescence, Moral Development and Classroom Management

Teaching Challenges: Internet Plagiarism, Academic Honesty, and Educational Technology

Student Level: High School

Ms. Clarice Benton has been teaching high school science for close to fifteen years. For the past couple of years, she has enjoyed teaching tenth-grade environmental science, and as she concludes the day's lesson unit in her second-period Earth/Science class she asks the students to move into their groups. The groups have recently been assigned a group project that asks students to discuss the large-scale environmental impacts resulting from human activity, including oil spills, runoff, greenhouse gases, ozone depletion, and surface and groundwater pollution. Ms. Benton asks that the groups begin planning their projects.

While Ms. Benton is circulating to answer questions, she stops at one group who have their hands up for her attention. "Ms. Benton, I am confused," Marissa begins. "I have been following along with the reading and your lessons, but I just don't get how to put it all together and see the long-term picture at work here. Does that make sense? I understand what you were saying about pollution and oil spills, but I am not sure how to pull it all together and write about consequences for long-term environmental impact and especially the ozone. And I really don't understand what they mean about the 'greenhouse effect.'"

Ms. Benton takes a moment to best consider her response. She understands that many students struggle with a more theoretical discussion of the profound effects on populations and ecosystem processes while using the more

11

strategic and complex reasoning the project demands. However, before Ms. Benton can respond, another member in this group becomes very animated in responding. "Marissa, it is so important we find ways to build a healthy and sustainable environment for future generations as well as habitat conservation for our wildlife. This summer I plan to volunteer with an organization committed to environmental conservation locally. Ms. Benton, I love this project!" exclaims Courtney.

Ms. Benton acknowledges Courtney's interest and briefly inquires as to her summer plans. She then returns to answering Marissa's question before reminding them both to also review the online resource she recently shared. Before leaving the group, she takes one more opportunity to engender some enthusiasm for what she considers one of the great questions in environmental science. She knows that sometimes the information that students discover for themselves is what stays with them the longest.

Ms. Benton then overhears comments at another table that concern her. Some students are unhappy with the assignment and somehow don't see the meaningfulness of the exercise. One of Ms. Benton's top students, Brittney, is saying, "It's not like I am going to be an environmental scientist, and it looks like this project is going to take way too much of my time. But colleges really care about how you do in your science classes. I have to get into one of my A-list schools!" Ms. Benton is stopped by a student asking a question about using the restroom, but continues to overhear the group's conversation.

Samantha replies, "I don't see the point either; I have two other projects in other classes that count for so much of my grade. Besides, it's not like I am understanding it all; it's like going over my head, you know? But I like Ms. Benton. She is so sweet, and I wouldn't want to hurt her feelings. So of course I'll do the project, but I am not even sure when I will find time to get it all done. Plus, we need this class to graduate. Ugh! My parents are always on my case about my grades even though I get like all As and Bs!"

Brittney makes a more alarming comment. "Maybe I will just use some of this," as she points to the tablet she is working on and makes a half-hearted laugh. Samantha interjects, "You can't just use that; you have to summarize and put it in your own words, or you will get into a mess of trouble." Brittney begins to tell her not to be ridiculous and informs her in a condescending tone that "doesn't she know everybody does it" at some point or another. "This isn't even plagiarism, Samantha, because there is no author listed on the website. So it is like common knowledge or something. Plus, I'm like an A student; no one would suspect me."

By this time, the teacher has made it back to the group and asks how they are doing so far. "We are doing OK, Ms. Benton; we will make sense of it," Samantha replies. "Great!" Ms. Benton notes. "So let me see what you are working on so far. Have you found a great website?" As Ms. Benton looks at the website with the girls, she tries to applaud their use of finding relevant information.

She also drops some hints about how to cite such a tricky site since no author is listed and reminds them how to integrate and evaluate multiple sources of information presented in diverse formats and media to best address any scientific problem. She answers all of their questions fully, hoping a crisis has been averted, and moves on to circulate until the period ends.

A couple of days later, Ms. Benton is in the hall between class periods on her way to her lunch period when she overhears Marissa asking Brittney questions about the science project. Marissa seems really distraught over the project. "I just don't get it. I am desperate! Any chance you can help me this weekend get a grip on this project?" Brittney responds, "Yeah, sure. I don't even know how I am going to find the time with all my other deadlines. But we can work on it together this weekend. We gotta stick together and help each other out. I am supposed to come up with the first part for my group anyway. I think I know of an easy way to put a paper together."

Ms. Benton is quite alarmed as to what this "easy way" is after overhearing Brittney's comments over the past couple of days. She decides it might be time to have a discussion on academic honesty in her class that could include adding some online tutorials as part of the project.

As she makes her way to the faculty lounge for lunch, she decides to get the opinion of one of her colleagues. Without mentioning names, she shares what she has overheard. Her colleague, Keith, shakes his head as he finishes a half of his sandwich. He appears to share some of the same frustration she herself has over the increasing issue of plagiarism in the high school ages. Keith commiserates, "Listen, Clarice, I believe that most kids try to do the right thing. And most are under immense pressure to get into the more competitive colleges. But I don't get how they don't realize exactly what constitutes plagiarism or even seem aware of our school's policy regarding academic honesty."

Clarice agrees. "Exactly! I have one student who seems to think of it as a way of just 'collecting information,' and they don't understand you have to give credit for someone else's ideas as well as their words. They don't grasp the concept of intellectual property, paraphrasing, or proper citation."

Keith responds, "You're right!" and begins to get even more animated. "One clear tip-off that they are cutting and pasting and trying to pass it off as their own work is when students ask me for help because they can't change the color of the text or reformat the margins. On the other hand, there are some tech-savvy students who are accustomed to downloading music and file sharing and therefore feel their teachers lack their level of technical sophistication when it comes to the Internet. There even seems to be some very bright students who take pride in beating the system and getting away with it!"

Clarice nods to her colleague. She now realizes just how complicated a problem this has become due to the advances in technology. She offers that as a faculty they should discuss this issue at one of the next meetings since a consistent message and policy are likely the best prevention. However, she needs to get to her next class. She thanks Keith for the information and lending an ear.

At the end of the week, Ms. Benton has just wrapped up her final class of the day and sits down to put together ideas for the online tutorial on the science project. This will includes not only important science content but also information on proper citation and reference to the school's Academic Policy. Before she begins, one of her students from her second-period class stops in. Martin relates how he overheard a couple of students in his class discussing copying a paper off the Internet. Martin complains to her that "it is simply not fair to the rest of us students when cheaters get a higher grade on a plagiarized paper while I spend long hours coming up with something on my own! It's not right! What are you going to do about this Ms. Benton? I hope something! Because it sure isn't fair to the rest of us."

DISCUSSION QUESTIONS

1. Cognitive Development in Adolescence
   a. According to Piaget, identify the stage of cognitive development students are likely to be in. Discuss challenges they might experience with abstract or hypothetico-deductive reasoning.
   b. How often do high school students struggle with (independent) problem solving and complex scientific thinking? How might this offer a platform for cheating to occur?
   c. What role does idealistic thinking play in adolescences' cognitive development, and how can teachers harness students' passion in environmental education?
   d. What role might adolescent egocentrism play in instances of cheating in the classroom?
   e. Discuss brain development during adolescence. How does ongoing development in the prefrontal cortex influence adolescences' decision making and judgment during stressful situations?

2. Moral Development
   a. According to Kohlberg's theory of moral development, determine the level and the stage Brittney is functioning in. Support your answer with examples from the case. What roles do peer approval, group norms, and peer pressure play?

   b. Imagine that this situation occurred in your classroom; generate examples of developmentally appropriate strategies for handling Internet plagiarism.

3. Internet Plagiarism
   a. What is intellectual property? When should students be introduced to the notion of Internet plagiarism?
   b. What are fair consequences for catching students who have engaged in Internet plagiarism? What should be considered? Is it grounds for failing grades? Suspension? Expulsion? Should there be a permanent mark in their records?
   c. How prevalent are paper-buying practices? How easy is it for students to access websites that freely offer subpar essays (but charge for those of more quality)?

4. Cheating Prevention
   a. How can teachers help students who feel they don't have enough time or are unprepared to write a paper on their own?
   b. How can teachers and schools help students who face demanding standards, pressure to earn top grades for admittance to competitive colleges, and a culture that potentially encourages "success at any cost"?
   c. What should be included in a school's academic honesty policy? What are clear expectations for academic integrity?
   d. Should a school consider using plagiarism detection services?
   e. How might carefully crafted assignments help prevent plagiarism? Would assignments that ask students to link classical literature to more current events help minimize the tendency to cheat? What about cycling the use of assignments so they are at least slightly changed each year?

Case 3

Academic Honesty

Suggested Theories: Moral Development, Social Development, Cognitive
Development, Behavioral Theory, Social Cognitive Theory, and Motivation
Teaching Challenges: Plagiarism and Cheating Prevention, Peer Rivalry, and
Social Adjustment
Student Level: Middle School

Neil has just begun genetics in his seventh-grade advanced biology class,
and he is really looking forward to studying this because he has heard
Mr. Wright makes it really fun. As he heads to his seat, Neil greets his classmates—some students are chatting with each other while others are on their
phones. Mr. Wright begins the class by opening up the presentation for his
lecture and asks that all students put their phones away for the remainder of
the class. Neil silences his phone as he slides it into his backpack, but many
other students keep their phones hidden yet within their reach.

At the end of class, Neil feels lost. He is not catching on to Mr. Wright's
explanations on mapping chromosomes as well as he thought he would. Neil
continues to feel lost in Mr. Wright's class all week, and he is stunned when
he earns a 62 percent on his first test. Neil's best subject is science, and he
has never earned such a low score before.

As Neil walks to his next class, his phone vibrates in his pocket with an
incoming text from his friend Ana Julia, who is also in Mr. Wright's class.

Ana Julia: *Hey, how'd you do on the test?* Neil: *Not good, you?* Ana Julia:
*Oh no! I got a 98. You can always join our study group. Still meeting at my
house day before tests.* Neil: *Thanks, but can't miss soccer practice.* Neil ends
before putting his phone away and enters his next class.

When Neil gets home that afternoon, his father asks him about the test and
is not pleased to hear his score. "You know, Neil, this is how your sister got

17

started down the path she is on today. First, she failed a test, then a major project, soon it was the class, and then she couldn't catch up anymore, so she gave up and quit school. Is this how you want to end up?" his father says angrily. "No, but . . . ," Neil stammers.

"But what?" his father interrupts and continues visibly upset. "I tell you, Neil, I am not accepting any of this nonsense from you. You are going to be the first one in this family to get a scholarship and go to a good college, so bring up that grade or you will be quitting all extracurricular activities and getting rid of that phone too! I told your mother I thought you should be spending more time studying and less time on other things. Maybe now she'll stop being so soft and understand that her trying to be your best friend is getting nowhere. I want to see that grade go up, you hear?" "Yes, I hear," Neil answers with a sigh.

The next day in class, Mr. Wright assigns a genetics project that counts for 40 percent of his grade. As Neil looks over the assignment, he knows he must do well if he is to raise his grade. He feels a great deal of pressure to do well in school so he can please his father but also because he has a starting position on the soccer team. He knows both his coach and his team are counting on him, and that means doing well in school because athletes must be passing all their classes or they are ineligible to play.

Neil is so distracted that he runs right into his teammate Jeff as he enters the locker room for practice that afternoon. Jeff is an eighth grader and the team's superstar. "Hey, man, what's up?" Jeff asks playfully. "Just got out of science and I was thinking about this big project we were just assigned," Neil replies as they get ready for practice. "Wait . . . don't tell me. You must be talking about old man Wright and his big genetics project!" Jeff says. "Yep, that's it," Neil answers. "Oh, man, I heard that project is so hard and he grades so strict; you are doomed! Get ready to flunk it, dude!"

"Great," mutters Neil, "I'm already in a world of trouble at home for not scoring very high on the test. My dad is going to be furious if I flunk the project too. My dad's been talking about me quitting the team; he thinks it is getting in the way of my schoolwork." "Wait, what?! Oh no, no, no, Neil! Man, that is really bad news and with the playoffs coming up! We have a real chance at the state championships this year!" Jeff explains incredulously and then asks, "Does your old man know how important you are to the team?"

"I don't know," Neil answers with a shrug, "and to be honest, I don't think he really cares. My dad doesn't really know how much playing means to me." Jeff cautiously asks, "Can your mom do something about it?" "I doubt it; my dad makes all the rules, and once he has his mind made up about something, my mom won't even try to change his mind," Neil answers. "You know what? I may be able to help you. I didn't have old man Wright, but my older brother had him. I could ask him if he still has the assignments saved on his computer—I mean it's not like Wright has changed anything. I hear he gives the same stuff year after year," Jeff says.

"But . . . I mean . . . wouldn't he remember the assignment? Wouldn't he know it isn't mine?" Neil asks nervously. "Nah, he's graded so many over the years that he's not gonna remember work from three years ago! Besides, he might be more suspicious if it was me 'cause he could remember that my brother was in his class, but you? He's not gonna put two and two together, man!" Jeff exclaims. "I'll ask my brother and if he still has it, I'll e-mail it to you. I know he got an A on it; he always gets As on everything. So by tomorrow you'll be on easy street."

Neil answers, "Well . . . I guess . . . I mean . . ." "Hey!" Jeff interrupts. "If you are going to be a little itty bitty coward about it, then forget it. Just flunk; it's your funeral, but don't say I didn't have your back, man!" "No, no, it's fine, Jeff. Thanks, man!" Neil says as the boys walk toward the field. "Don't mention it!" Jeff says and pats Neil's back jovially.

That evening, Jeff sends Neil his brother's assignment in an e-mail. As Neil looks at it he realizes this really is a perfect paper. It's no wonder Jeff's brother earned a near-perfect score! Neil's thoughts are interrupted when Jeff texts him.

Jeff: *You got it?* Neil: *Yeah, it's awesome but will take me a few days to rewrite it. Don't wanna have him think that it's not my work.* Jeff: *You worry too much; quit acting like such a loser, man. Everyone's done it at some point or another. Some buy papers. You wanna be off the team?* Neil: *Definitely not.* Jeff: *Wanna lose your social life?* Neil: *No, that would suck.* Jeff: *Man, you see who's having a party this weekend?* Neil: *Yeah, wouldn't want to miss it.* Jeff: *That's what I'm talking about; we'll all be there.*

Neil's and Jeff's texts quickly come to an end when Neil hears his father in the hallway and is sure he will come in his room to lecture him again. His father's latest sermon along with his texts to Jeff help Neil decide to make a few minor changes to Jeff's brother's assignment and submit it as his own. Now that he's made this decision, Neil feels a huge weight has been lifted off his shoulders; after all, his science grade will no longer be a problem he has to worry about.

The following week, when Neil walks in to Mr. Wright's class, he notices that something unusual is happening. He decides to ask Jamaad, who sits next to him. "What? You didn't hear what happened?" Jamaad asks surprised. "Nah, what's up?" Neil asks as he sits down. "It's all over social media, dude! Check your phone so you're not out of it. Word is that old man Wright is out for blood!" Jamaad says as he playfully slaps Neil on the arm.

"Oh yeah," Ana Julia sits down and joins their conversation. "I've been getting texts all morning! Looks like someone in this class forged a paper or something, and Mr. Wright is beyond mad. He's wanting to make an example of whoever did this because he doesn't ever want it to happen again," Ana Julia says animatedly. "Wow, am I glad I decided not to skip class today; wouldn't want to miss this!" Jamaad exclaims.

However, before Neil has a chance to respond to his classmates, Mr. Wright comes in to the class accompanied by Mrs. Goodgen, the assistant principal. Mr. Wright turns on the projector screen that is linked to his computer, and Neil's assignment appears on the screen in front of the class. Neil is astounded; the class is quiet except for a few students' whispers.

"Well," says Mr. Wright in a stern tone, "does anyone recognize this paper?" All of the students are silent. "This paper," Mr. Wright continues, "was turned in by one of the students in this class to be graded as their original work," Mr. Wright pauses. "However, this paper is not that student's work; this paper was turned in three years ago by another student who received a very high grade and who should remain anonymous." Neil doesn't dare move, but he can see his classmates turning to each other with puzzled expressions. "So," Mr. Wright says sternly before continuing, "I would like the student who committed the offense to stand and acknowledge their actions; after all, they definitely think they are so very smart to get away with this. I want this student to apologize to the class and to me for their behavior before Mrs. Goodgen escorts them out."

A few whispers can be heard, but no one risks speaking. Neil is shocked and begins to feel sick. "Well, well, well, it seems that the guilty party doesn't want to come forward on their own accord, so I will have to identify him to the class," Mr. Wright says and walks over to where Neil is sitting. "Neil, I thought you would like the chance to explain to all of us why you turned in someone else's project as your own, as I said you obviously thought you were so smart that you didn't need to actually do the work, only forge it." Neil begins to speak, but he can't; he can feel his face turning red, and he can hear his classmates murmuring all around him.

Neil wishes he could disappear into the desk and the entire situation would cease to exist. Seeing that Neil is choosing to remain quiet, Mrs. Goodgen taps him on the shoulder and motions for Neil to come with her. As they walk in silence to her office, Mrs. Goodgen informs Neil that Mr. Wright has requested a conference with Neil's parents before he can be allowed back in to his class, and the conference has been set up for the next day.

After school, Mr. Wright stops by Mrs. Goodgen's office to let her know that Neil's parents have confirmed that they will be coming in tomorrow morning to discuss the situation with their son. However, judging the nature of the offense, he asks that she be present. "Sure, I'm glad to sit in," Mrs. Goodgen says. "I have to say I am a bit surprised by Neil's behavior because he hasn't been in any kind of trouble before and he has a high grade point average. I just don't understand why students take such a risk when they are well aware of the consequences." Mr. Wright nods as he leans against the doorway of her office.

"I agree; I did not expect this from Neil. How did your conversation go with him?" Mr. Wright asks. "Well, we spoke only briefly while he waited for his older sister to pick him up," Mrs. Goodgen paused before continuing, "but he did not take responsibility for his actions. Instead, he made various excuses, from claiming he didn't know that what he did would be considered cheating to claiming he did it because he is stressed and this is what everyone does." Mr. Wright shakes his head in disbelief as he and Mrs. Goodgen continue their chat.

DISCUSSION QUESTIONS

1. Moral Development
   a. According to Kohlberg's theory of moral development, determine the level and stage that Neil is functioning in. Discuss examples in the case that speak to his reasoning at the level and stage chosen.
   b. According to Kohlberg's theory of moral development, determine the level and stage that Mr. Wright is functioning in. Support your answer with examples from the case.
   c. According to Kohlberg's theory of moral development, determine the level and stage that Jeff and Neil are functioning in. Support your answer with examples from the case.
   d. From the perspective of Piaget's theory of moral development, at what stage is Mr. Wright functioning in? How is that indicative in his actions in the case?
   e. Imagine that this situation occurred in your classroom; generate examples of developmentally appropriate strategies that you could use for managing plagiarism.

2. Socioemotional Development
   a. According to Baumrind's parenting styles, identify the style of parenting exhibited by Neil's mother and father. Drawing on the research on parenting styles, how can parenting styles impact a child's behavior—both academically and socially?
   b. Explain how peers play a role in this case. Justify how peer pressure and acceptance played a part in Neil's behavior.
   c. Speculate how adolescent friendships, peer rivalry, social adjustment, and social development in general can be affected by students' involvement in social media and their constant cell phone use? How can increasing interactions in the online environment help to shape adolescents' social development?

d. How can Neil's choice and the consequences of his choice impact his self-esteem and self-concept? How can these self-constructs be affected by a teen's constant interaction with social media?

e. Discuss how you could apply Bronfenbrenner's ecological systems theory to this case. Which of Bronfenbrenner's ecological systems would be most influential in this case?

f. Determine how Neil's use of excuses to explain his actions rather than accepting blame has affected his perception of the situation as well as his capacity for moral development. How can teachers assist students in learning to take responsibility for their actions?

3. Cognitive Development in Adolescence

a. What stage of Piaget's theory of cognitive development is Neil functioning in? Support with examples from the case.

b. Discuss how an adolescent's thinking and reasoning might play a part in Neil's poor decision making in this case.

c. What role may Piaget's idealistic thinking play in adolescences' cognitive development, and how can teachers assist students to become more realistic?

d. Explain how Elkind's adolescent egocentrism could be of significance when understanding the reasons for moral decisions, specifically cheating in the classroom? Discuss ways that teachers can assist students in reducing their adolescent egocentrism.

e. Discuss the role that social media plays in adolescents' cognitive development. How may it impede, rather than assist, adolescents' cognitive growth?

4. Behavioral and Cognitive Approaches

a. Identify a potential classical conditioning example that is taking place in the case. Be sure to identify the unconditioned stimulus, unconditioned response, conditioned stimulus, and conditioned response.

b. How could a teacher extinguish a potentially harmful conditioned response? Could stimulus desensitization be used?

c. Describe the type of punishment that Mr. Wright used in this case. Outline the advantages and disadvantages that using punishment poses for the classroom environment.

d. Discuss other behavioral theories that could have been employed in this case.

e. Explain how this case can be analyzed using Bandura's social cognitive theory. How is Neil's self-efficacy challenged as a result of his poor performance? How could a student's self-regulation prevent poor decision making?

5. Motivation
   a. Describe how Neil's actions in this case align with Maslow's hierarchy of needs. Support your answers with examples from the case.
   b. Speculate how Neil's behavior could be explained both from an intrinsic and extrinsic motivational perspective. What are the drawbacks of extrinsic motivation?
   c. According to achievement motivation, explain whether Mr. Wright's classroom environment is more conducive to mastery orientations or to performance orientations.
   d. Explain events in the case using Bandura's self-efficacy as a motivational construct. In general, describe the importance of motivation for academic achievement.

6. Plagiarism and Cheating Prevention: Teachers and Schools
   a. What types of school services or assistance can schools and teachers offer student-athletes who devote much of their after-school time in practice?
   b. How can teachers and schools help adolescents to better handle the stress of succeeding in a competitive world of demanding schedules and pressure for future college acceptance?
   c. Outline ideas about the consequences and expectations that schools should clearly communicate in their student manuals regarding academic honesty. Should plagiarism detection services be employed?
   d. Explain how refraining from recycling the use of assignments from year to year and creating assignments that cannot easily be copied may help to prevent or discourage plagiarism.
   e. Generate fair and reasonable consequences for students who are caught cheating at both the individual teacher and school-wide levels.

Case 4

Cyberbullying and Adolescent Identity

Suggested Theories: Identity Development, Cognitive Development, and Moral
   Development
Teacher Challenges: Social-Emotional Well-Being, Social Media and
   Cyberbullying
Student Level: High School

Eleventh graders in Mrs. Torres's health class are presenting their research projects on their assigned topic. Today's group, Isabella, Sierra, Tarik, and Mauricio, will be presenting on healthy living. Mrs. Torres is happy to see that the students are all prepared and begin their presentation by discussing the Food Guide Pyramid and the data they compiled on dietary guidelines. Their presentation has sparked a class-wide discussion centered around weight and body image. "I think it is not fair that the media is obsessed with showing images of skinny girls. TV, magazines, social media—it's every-where and I mean it's not real life," Tarik says.

Many students voice their agreement. "Yeah, and they don't eat much! And the guys? The media is all about perfect physiques with six-pack abs. What is that all about? Not real," adds Josephine. The discussion continues with Mrs. Torres pointing to data in the students' presentation that indeed shows the class how difficult it can be for some people to fit into the stereotypical physical ideal that media sources push as being the norm for adolescents. The students end their presentation by discussing various ways to prepare healthy meals, which include all the food groups, citing various websites they researched that support their claims.

Mrs. Torres is certainly pleased to see how well the students have been cov-ering the topics they were assigned, which she specifically crafted to address many of the struggles she believes adolescents are confronted with. These issues range from peer pressure to body image and fashion trends, to dating and intimacy, to drugs and alcohol and future careers. Mrs. Torres ends the class by saying, "Wonderful job today, everyone. Tomorrow's group four will be discussing careers in health. I am looking forward to hearing their work!"

As her students exit the classroom, Mrs. Torres overhears Isabella and Sierra talking quietly. "Sierra, just ignore the nasty text like those others she sent. You know Jenna and her horrible friends are just trying to get to you. You are not fat. Do not let her make you feel bad about yourself. She's been like that since you started dating Ian. If you ask me I think she liked him and is just jealous he liked you instead of her," Isabella says. Sierra is visibly upset but doesn't answer her friend as the girls leave the classroom.

Mrs. Torres wonders how long Sierra has been receiving negative text messages; Jenna has not demonstrated any animosity toward Sierra in class. She makes a mental note to check with other teachers to see whether they have noticed signs that Sierra has been receiving repeated text messages and thus being bullied.

Isabella and Sierra are talking while they walk toward the baseball field. Isabella puts her arm around her friend and says, "Thanks for staying with me to watch Grant's baseball practice. You know how strict my parents are. They would never let me stay after school to see Grant's practice, and they would absolutely freak out if they knew I was going over to his house again today."

"Sure, Isa, no problem," Sierra says as they choose a spot to sit on the bleachers that overlook the baseball team's practice. Isabella rolls her eyes in annoyance. "I mean I really don't see what the big deal is; I'm taking the contraceptive pill, so it's not like there's anything to worry about. I mean I can't get an STD or get pregnant because we are totally protected with me on the pill, but still you know them."

"Oh yeah, I mean you are totally protected if you are on the pill," Sierra says in agreement.

"Grant's house is the best place to hang out because his parents are never around, and when they are they let him do just about anything he wants to do as long as he doesn't bother them. Last week, some of his older sister's friends showed up, and they had alcohol with them," Isabella says in a low voice.

"Whoa. Really? Did you drink?" Sierra asks surprised.

"Well I would have looked pretty stupid if I hadn't, don't you think? I mean I don't want Grant to think that I can't hang like all of them. It's just like for prom Grant gets to stay out all night, but I am supposed to be in by curfew . . . not going to happen. I'm going to stay out all night and of course I'll get grounded after, but whatever, nothing new there," Isabella says annoyed. Sierra nods and puts her hand on her friend's arm empathetically. "I feel bad always lying to them, but you can't discuss anything with them. All conversations lead to statements like 'as long as you live under my roof, you will abide by my rules,'" Isabella says with a sigh.

"Yeah, that's tough," Sierra responds sympathetically and adds, "but they are still OK with you spending the night on Saturday?"

"Yeah! And we are so going to Lebron's party! With your parents all the way across the city at your dad's work party, they won't know if we come in after curfew."

Sierra nods excitedly, and the girls move to discuss the latest prom fashions while looking at their classmates' social media posts on their phones. Both girls' express apprehension over ensuring that they buy dresses that will be met with their peers' approval, even if it isn't always what they would have thought to buy themselves.

The next day in Mrs. Torres's class, the students presenting on careers in health have begun their presentation by recognizing several professions in the health care field and identifying various effective characteristics of health care providers. The class then moves to discuss these occupations as possible career paths, and several students express interest but many remain quiet. In an effort to get all students involved in the discussion, Mrs. Torres decides to call on students. "Mauricio, do you find any of the discussed occupations interesting?"

"I am not sure, Mrs. Torres, because I had not known as much about them until today, but I think so," Mauricio says. Mrs. Torres nods and calls on a few more students who have varying opinions on future occupations. "OK, I think we have time for a couple more comments before class ends," Mrs. Torres says as she calls on Isabella, whose hand is raised.

"Well, to be honest, Mrs. Torres, I do not know in the least what I want to do or where I want to go to school. I mean Grant does; he's already been accepted and even knows his major, so I could join him there or . . . well, I want to do something that deals with fashion, or . . . maybe music, or possibly even travel to Europe for a while. I think it would be totally cool to just wander around all those different countries!" Isabella exclaims excitedly as some of her classmates nod their heads in agreement. Mrs. Torres knows that Isabella's confession regarding her future is common among her students as they work to form their identity.

Mrs. Torres then turns her attention to Sierra, happy to see that she is choosing to participate. Sierra is always very reserved in class discussions and shies away from conversations; however, none of her other teachers had noticed anything amiss about her behavior—they all agreed that she was just shy and kept to herself. "Sierra what did you have to add?" Mrs. Torres asks.

"Oh, um, well . . . I will be going to school for accounting because my parents have always dreamed we will work together in our family business and um . . . I'm good with numbers; I mean I'm good at math, so it will be like no problem for me to breeze through a school nearby while I work part-time for my parents, which is you know . . . um good," Sierra answers hesitantly.

The bell rings indicating the end of class, and Mrs. Torres addresses the class. "Another fantastic presentation today and great participation. I encourage all of you to think about your future careers and research your options so you are well informed regardless of whether you are sure of what you want or still undecided. See you tomorrow!"

As the lunch period comes to an end, Isabella notices that Sierra is walking away very quickly. "What's that about?" Grant asks Isabella, motioning toward Sierra. "I'm not sure; looks like she is heading to the bathroom again," Isabella responds. She wonders if her friend is alright because she knows she got another mean text after health class today—this one ridiculed her for her career choices. In addition, Isabella has also noticed that Sierra has been excusing herself to use the bathroom after she eats; however, when Isabella has inquired about it, Sierra has either blamed it on a stomachache or the new diet she is on to lose weight before prom.

"Hmm, you think it has anything to do with all the mean comments that were all over social media after Saturday's party? I mean she's gotta be hurting; those remarks were vicious," Grant says. "Yeah, so typical of Jenna. I don't know why they just won't stop! Sierra refuses to talk about it," Isabella responds sadly. "It sucks. Remember when that happened to Bobby last year after homecoming?" Grant asks. "Oh yeah, it all ended up with some ugly fist fights," responds Isabella. Both Grant and Isabella agree that Sierra should tell someone that she is being bullied rather than hoping it will just stop.

Isabella wonders if perhaps she should talk to the school counselor about Sierra. But then again, what if Sierra gets angry with her for discussing her with the school counselor? No, she is probably overreacting; after all, Sierra is a smart girl and she must know what she is doing—it will all be alright. Things always have a way of working out.

A few weeks later as Mrs. Torres walks to her car she is reflecting on her students' health presentations now that they are finished. This was a new assignment she introduced this year to get students to take more interest in the class. She had noticed some students were frequently distracted and weren't bothering to take notes. Isabella, for example, consistently studied off others' notes. She'd arrange for them to take a picture of their class notes and send them to her, which would help explain Isabella's poor scores on the weekly quizzes.

Mrs. Torres realizes that her students' social life is at their forefront of their minds and unfortunately is often chosen over their academics. In the case of Isabella, Mrs. Torres has heard repeatedly of Isabella's involvement with a popular senior student who has recently asked her to prom, an honor that other students envy because Isabella is a junior and students often have to wait until they are seniors to attend. Suddenly, Mrs. Torres hears a student crying inside a car. "Isabella, what's wrong?" Mrs. Torres asks alarmed. "I just found out . . . I am pregnant, Mrs. Torres, and I don't know what am I going to do," Isabella says as she continues to sob.

DISCUSSION QUESTIONS

1. Identity Development
   a. According to Erikson's theory of psychosocial development, determine the stage that Isabella is functioning in. Discuss examples of how this is demonstrated in the case. How is she likely to resolve the crisis that occurs in this stage?
   b. From the perspective of Erikson's theory of psychosocial development, discuss how Sierra is developing an identity. What stage of Erikson's theory of psychosocial development is Sierra functioning in?
   c. How can teachers assist their students' development of identity? What examples of this were evident in the case?
   d. Explain, from Marcia's identity development, where each of the students is with respect to their identity status. How is that evident in the case?
   e. Discuss how each of the classifications of Marcia's identity statuses describe how a person's identity forms.

2. Socioemotional Development
   a. According to Baumrind's parenting styles, identify the style of parenting exhibited by Isabella's parents. How is the way that Isabella is being parented affected her behavior and identity? Is this different from Sierra's parents?
   b. According to Baumrind's parenting styles, identify the style of parenting that Grant's parents demonstrate. What effects is this style of parenting having on Grant and his older sister?
   c. Explain how peers play a role in this case. Justify how peer pressure and acceptance play a role in these students' behavior.
   d. Discuss how you could apply Bronfenbrenner's ecological systems theory to the students in this case. Which of Bronfenbrenner's ecological systems may best explain social development in this case?
   e. Speculate on how becoming a teenage mother would impact an adolescent's self-concept and self-esteem. Discuss the challenges that adolescent mothers face with regard to their academic future.

3. Social Media and Cyberbullying
   a. Discuss the dangers of cyberbullying. In what ways might social media serve as a platform for cyberbullying? What signs should teachers look for to help identify students who are being cyberbullied?

  b. How are friendships, peer rivalry, and social comparisons affected by adolescents' constant use of social media and cell phones? How can adolescents' identity be influenced by their constant interaction with social media?

  c. How do media use and chronic media multitasking on different technology media relate to feelings of social success and students' social well-being?

  d. Is increased social media use causing issues in students' social well-being, or are socially challenged adolescents drawn to spending more time plugged into multiple technologies?

  e. What is "Internet addiction"? What adolescent characteristics might indicate this phenomenon? What are its consequences for face-to-face friendships? Outline resources that schools can provide to educate adolescents about the dangers of cyberbullying, sexually transmitted diseases, pregnancy, and the hazards of alcohol and drugs.

4. Cognitive Development in Adolescence

  a. According to Piaget, identify the stage of cognitive development students are likely to be in. Support your answer with examples from the case.

  b. Identify instances of Piaget's concepts of assimilation and accommodation. At the end of the case, how has Isabella been thrown into a state of disequilibrium? How will she regain equilibrium?

  c. What role may Piaget's idealistic thinking play in adolescents' cognitive development, and how can teachers assist students to become more realistic rather than idealistic?

  d. Explain how Elkind's adolescent egocentrism is evident in this case. Discuss ways that teachers can assist students in reducing their adolescent egocentrism.

  e. Discuss the role that social media plays in adolescents' cognitive development. How may it impede rather than promote adolescents' cognitive development?

5. Moral Development

  a. According to Kohlberg's theory of moral development, determine the level and the stage that Isabella is functioning in. Support your answer with examples from the case. What roles do peer approval, group norms, and peer pressure play in Isabella's choosing to lie to her parents?

  b. According to Kohlberg's theory of moral development, determine the level and the stage that Sierra is functioning in. How is her friendship with Isabella affecting her moral development? Support your answer with examples from the case.

c. How are the students' level and stage of moral development, according to Kohlberg, possibly affecting their identity development?

d. Summarize how Gilligan's theory sheds light on the events presented in this case.

e. Distinguish between Kohlberg's and Gilligan's views of moral reasoning. Demonstrate the importance of moral reasoning as well as how it may affect behavioral outcomes.

Part II

INDIVIDUAL DIFFERENCES
AND DIVERSITY

Case 5

Gender Equity

Encouraging Female Students in Science

Suggested Theories: Gender Roles, Gender Differences, Socialization of Gender
Roles, and Equitable Teaching Practices
Teacher Challenges: Sexism, Gender Stereotypes, Adolescent Behaviors
Student Level: High School

Rosa Mendez is in her second year of teaching life science at Culbertson
High School. She is very happy with her teaching position since she has
always loved science and she finds working with high schoolers to be very
rewarding. Mrs. Mendez's fourth-period tenth-grade class begins entering the
room and taking their seats. Mrs. Mendez greets them, and as the bell rings
signaling the beginning of the period Mrs. Mendez reminds them to silence
their phones and put them away so they are ready to learn.

Mrs. Mendez addresses her class. "Hello, class. I wanted to take some time
today to discuss exam grades. Many students have been consistently earning
low scores on tests, and I am concerned especially since on class activities
and reviews there doesn't seem to be any problems. I hope that in talking as a
class we will be able share concerns that will in turn give me a better understanding of what may be occurring." It is clear as Mrs. Mendez looks around
the room that many students share in her concern while others seem unfazed.
Hands begin raising for a chance to speak, but before Mrs. Mendez can call
on a student, Vincent, one of the students seated toward the front, speaks up
without waiting to be called on.

"Mrs. Mendez, no way that I did bad! I mean no way! The team has the
lacrosse playoffs this weekend, and coach won't let anyone play that isn't
passing all subjects! I cannot deal with this now!" Several other male students
voice similar concerns. "Yeah, Mrs. Mendez! Not possible any of us could
have done badly because that test was so easy! And we studied—we met

at Frankie's house because we know we got playoffs," Gustavo says loudly while motioning to the group of boys he is seated with.

Mrs. Mendez nods her head and says calmly, "I never said that any of you in particular did poorly, gentlemen, nor am I speaking about any one student in particular. This is an informative conversation so I can get better insight about what may have happened." Frankie, who is seated next to Gustavo and Vincent, says without raising his hand for permission to speak, "I mean no offense, Mrs. Mendez, but this is a waste of time! I like this class, but I mean, why don't you just talk to the students who we all know are doing badly because they just can't do science?" A chorus of agreements are heard around the room, and now students are expressing fear over their grades affecting their playing lacrosse or offering up excuses for their possible poor performance—such as having other assignments or tests in other classes or extracurricular obligations.

Mrs. Mendez sighs and realizes that this conversation is not going in the direction that she had hoped. "Listen class, I am well aware of the athletic policies, and my purpose here is not to cause fear nor is it to hear excuses. Now, I know that many of you studied and that many of you did well. However, I wondered if all of you are consistently following all of the helpful tips that we discussed during the review and that I have listed on the study guide. Did you all spend time going over the reading assignments and lab activities? Did you all do the practice questions or any of the other review items on the textbook's website as I suggested?"

Mrs. Mendez looks around the room at her students. Many of them shift uneasily in their seats; others look at other students, and some refuse to make eye contact with her. Mrs. Mendez decides to focus her attention on the back of the room where a large group of girls are sitting together. The girls are quietly chatting among themselves; however, none of these students have contributed to the discussion.

"Ladies in the back, would you like to share your thoughts with the rest of the class with regard to the exams?" One of the students mumbles something under her breath that Mrs. Mendez cannot hear, and a few others look decidedly uncomfortable. However, one of the students, Hannah, raises her hand, and Mrs. Mendez acknowledges her to speak. "Well, Mrs. Mendez, I don't know about the rest of the class, but I think the tests are really hard. It takes me forever to get through reading all this stuff, and then I still have to make time to sit down and answer all these questions you give us. And the online reviews are tough to get through if you don't really understand the material completely."

Mrs. Mendez sees that there are many students who are nodding their heads in agreement. "I understand what you are saying, Hannah," Mrs. Mendez says, "but the homework and study exercises I assign are not unrealistically long, and they are consistent with the curriculum and grade level."

Ileana, who is seated next to Hannah, looks around with a degree of uncertainty but raises her hand. After receiving Mrs. Mendez's recognition to speak, she says, "Well . . . umm . . . it's not really the amount of work that is the problem, Mrs. Mendez. It's the work itself that is really hard. Um, like last week, when we were using the microscopes, I didn't get enough time to view all the plant and animal cells we were discussing, and that hurt me when I tried to . . . um answer the questions later . . . and well I did a lot of guessing . . . and obviously I guessed wrong . . . on many of the questions." Ileana finishes and looks around shyly to see how others have reacted to her statement.

Much to Mrs. Mendez's surprise, she sees that many of the students agree and that the majority of these students are girls. Mrs. Mendez feels a certain degree of apprehension at what she is discovering since she had not thought to look at the students' test scores in relation to their gender. Another of the girls seated in the large group in the back, Lydia, raises her hand to speak, and Mrs. Mendez calls on her. "I think the information on the test reviews is great . . . but, well, I don't think I get as much out of them because it moves too rapidly. It's like the same students answer all the questions, and they do it fast and so I don't have time to think. I end up just writing down the answer and later trying to memorize it . . . which doesn't always work."

Mrs. Mendez once again notices that the majority of the students agreeing with Lydia are girls. Suddenly, Shane startles the class by saying loudly, "Well, we can't help it if some of you don't know this stuff and then on top of it you are S-L-O-W." Soon the class erupts with loud chatter, and Vincent, making a gesture toward the back of the room where the majority of the female students are seated, says, "I mean really, it's not like everyone here is going to be a scientist! C'mon, ladies. It's a guy's job anyway." Mrs. Mendez settles the class down and makes a few notes on her planner to consider later while letting her students know she has heard all their concerns and will get back to them with any changes once she has had time to consider the situation.

"Alright, class, let's move on to today's activity, which is something new, and I am excited to see how well it works! Please look at the handout I am passing out. You will see that I have placed you all in groups so that you may work on the different habitats. Your assignment consists of estimating the kinds of plant and animal life native to your assigned habitat. You will see there are various materials along the countertops that will aid you in this assignment. I have also given you various websites to start off your research, but I do want you to find your own and not just use the ones I have given you.

"Based on today's discussions, I want to ensure that all of you are being considerate of your peers and that everyone is getting a chance on the computers, equipment, and so on. All students should be patient in allowing others in the group to arrive at the answers. I will be circulating around the room to answer questions, so, folks, be sure to ask me!" The students all move around the room finding their groups and settling down to work.

Mrs. Mendez's teaching assistant, Ginger Connolly, arrives and waves from the back of the class where she is storing her purse and lunch in Mrs. Mendez's armoire before she walks over to join in the activity. Ms. Connolly is studying to be a teacher at a nearby university and works at the school part-time as a teaching assistant. Ms. Connolly claps her hands excitedly and exclaims, "Wow, look at these kids! I can practically see learning take placing! This is what school is all about. . . . You sure work wonders with them!"

Mrs. Mendez smiles at the compliment and thanks Mrs. Connolly. Both Mrs. Mendez and Ms. Connolly circulate around the room to guide students who need assistance and to ensure students are on track. Soon, however, a commotion erupts in one of the groups, and Mrs. Connolly, who is closer to the group, walks over to handle the situation. "Stop, Vincent! You are being such a jerk!" one of the girls in his group says in a low voice. However, Vincent is clearly enjoying teasing her much to the great amusement of the other guys in his group.

"Seriously, Ms. Cheerleader, stop taking so long on this. You know you're hot! No one cares that you suck at science! I know we don't!" Vincent says softly in a conspiratorial tone as he quietly laughs and claps his friend's back who is seated next to him. All of the students in the group laugh, including the girl Vincent was speaking to. Outbursts like these are not uncommon, and Mrs. Mendez knows that Ms. Connolly will handle the disruption or will signal for her if she needs assistance.

Last week, Mrs. Mendez had a similar situation occur where a few of the boys appeared to be teasing a few of the girls. Mrs. Mendez kept them all after class, where the boys begrudgingly admitted they were just flirting and apologized. The girls all agreed that was what happened, but Mrs. Mendez still reminded them all of the consequences of class disruptions and that they were to keep their social agendas out of the classroom. Keeping in mind what some of the female students had mentioned earlier about not having had enough time to complete activities, Mrs. Mendez pays close attention to how the groups are sharing the materials. She notes that it is primarily the female students writing the information on the report sheets and sorting through the information while the male students are searching the Internet, actively searching for data in the classroom bins and sharing the results.

Mrs. Mendez also notices that the composition of some of the groups is not heterogeneous with regard to gender or ability although she randomly assigned students to groups. It looks like there are groups that consist of more males than females and vice versa and that some of the students who have consistently achieved higher scores are together, and the same is true for students who have achieved lower scores. Mrs. Mendez composed the groups prior to her becoming aware of some of the issues that may have affected the test scores; however, now that she is considering these effects, she makes a note on her planner to further examine group placement with regard to gender and ability.

As the students pack up their belongings and begin making their way to the door of the class, Mrs. Mendez overhears Hannah and Ileana talking from her post by the door collecting papers. "How do you like your group?" Ileana asks Hannah. "They're OK I guess, a little noisy. . . . I definitely feel lost again today, but I'm not too worried because I meet with my science tutor today after school, and he'll go over it all with me. If it wasn't for him I'd fail for sure," Hannah says in earnest. "Oh, you're so lucky. . . . And he's nice?" Ileana asks. "Yeah, he's great! My parents are friendly with his parents. He is in college and is majoring in one of the sciences . . . I forget which. Maybe I can ask him if he can tutor you too."

Ileana responds kindly, "That would be awesome, but my parents wouldn't go for that because my brother is supposed to help me; you know how crazy smart he is . . . but of course he has zero patience with me and thinks I am just dumb. So sometimes it's better to study by myself." Another girl, Zahra, joins in asking them how they did on the test, and the girls discuss that their grades were not as high as they had hoped. "Hey, did you end up going over to Gustavo's and studying with the lacrosse guys? Did it help you at all?" Hannah asks Zahra, who is dating Gustavo.

"Nah," Zahra answers, "I reviewed with them a little, but then Gustavo and I went to see that new extreme sports movie he's been dying to see." Hannah rolls her eyes at Zahra and says, "I thought you didn't want to see that movie. What happened to telling him so?" The girls are interrupted as Gustavo grabs Zahra's hand and pulls her to him so he can put his arm around her as they walk out of the class, their voices trailing off as they walk down the hallway.

The next period is Mrs. Mendez's planning period, and both she and Ms. Connolly are chatting as they finish inputting grades into the school's online gradebook. "You know the kids seemed to really enjoy today's activity. You are so innovative—always changing up your instruction! Are you doing this type of learner-centered instruction in all your classes?" Ms. Connolly asks.

"Well, thank you, I surely appreciate you saying so," Mrs. Mendez says kindly. "I do always try to infuse learner-centered practices into my lessons because I want to engage and motivate all of my students to see the importance of science. I am happy that the lessons are going so well; however, I am concerned with some of the students' test grades. After talking to the students today, I went back and looked across my classes, and it appears that many of the female students are not performing at the level of my male students. In addition, I am now recalling conversations that I have had with several of my female students with regard to their grade, and the general feeling was that they did not expect to succeed in science or math because they are girls. I got the distinct feeling that many of their parents share these beliefs and hence set low expectations for their daughters in those subjects. One student recently shared with me that she'd never done as well on science fair experiments as her brothers but that it was alright because both she and her family accepted that she would not earn the high grades or the accolades that her brothers did in science."

Ms. Connolly doesn't seem surprised as she responds, "I know. I hear the same things as well. It's the same in my family. My dad and brother excel in math and science, whereas my mom says she has trouble balancing her checkbook. My mom was so proud of me for working here with you rather than with the English class I had applied for. I mean girls in general are bound to have more trouble with science and math. I try to help them every chance I get, but some just cannot get it. I feel so bad for them. When I work with them in here I make sure to give lots of encouragement for trying and tell them not to take their scores to heart—it's just part of being a girl! It's like when the boys get to playful teasing . . . I hear them and they don't mean anything by it other than to comment on how a girl looks. I mean after all boys will be boys." Before Mrs. Mendez has a chance to respond, the bell rings indicating the end of the period, and students in Mrs. Mendez's next class begin to walk in and take their seats.

Later that week, Rosa is chatting with other teachers in the teachers' lounge. "Lance, I am at my wit's end with some of my female students' performance. I just don't get it; they do well some of the time, but they also repeatedly fail or do poorly on the examinations. I have spent hours on lesson preparation, orderly lesson presentations, and homework assignments that incorporate higher order questions, yet many of my female students are struggling with their performances on exams. I am troubled by this because science is a part of STEM and there are so many opportunities for them to be a part of—both now and in their futures. I mean look at enrollment rates in undergraduate programs in science as well as careers such as science and engineering. Girls are underrepresented."

Lance, a veteran English teacher listens intently as he drinks his coffee, his lunch already finished and packed in his lunch bag. "Have you tried collaborative assignments? They tend to align better with females' learning styles, and it's beneficial for all students since they enjoy the social setting of learning as well as the chance to really roll up their sleeves and work with materials hands on. This can be especially effective if you balance out the groups so no one group has too many males or too many females—the same holds true for ability," Lance says reflectively before continuing. "You can try researching articles on gender theories and teaching strategies. As you learned from conversing with your students, there are always various viewpoints to consider! Perhaps now you will also want to reconsider your assessments."

Rosa eats her salad as she considers the valuable advice that Lance is imparting. Another teacher, Jennifer Matthews, who teaches history sits at their table with her lunch and joins their conversation adding that she too experiences gender-related concerns in her class.

Lance continues, saying, "You know it certainly is true that girls sometimes struggle with science concepts, but I have found that sometimes it is males who are at a disadvantage. Many of my male students struggle with their grammar skills, and it's even more of a concern now with the use of technology and grammar checks on word processing because it enables them to rely on these programs rather than learn the grammar skills."

Jennifer quickly responds, saying, "Lance, while I agree that males certainly can struggle with grammar and writing, everyone knows teachers characteristically spend more time with boys in the math and science areas! And it doesn't even stop there! Take a look at history. Do you have any idea how many hours I have spent trying to come up with materials that represent female accomplishments in history? What message are we sending when our female students don't see strong female role models?" Jennifer pauses before continuing. "The curriculum has always been biased in favor of boys! This is exactly why you see single-sex education becoming such a hot topic!"

Lance puts up his hands in mock defense. "I hear you, really I do, and I empathize. But my point is there are biases for both genders. Take a look at the area of language arts, for example. Male students consistently score lower than female students from elementary through high school, and boys are more frequently in need of remediation in reading. This raises serious concerns."

They all agree that these points that are being raised all have merit, and as the conversation continues, Rosa asks, "Do you all think that children being bombarded with gender stereotypes and information on traditional gender roles from a young age could have an effect?" Both Lance and Jennifer nod in agreement.

Jennifer gets up to throw away the trash from her finished lunch and says, "Sure! I think so. In fact gender stereotypes and biases are everywhere you look—from the media to the Internet to the books they read. Lance, isn't it true that in typical fiction, the titles and lead characters are more often than not males?"

Lance contemplates this question and answers, "Truth is, evidence of gender bias exists against both males and females. My belief as an old sage who has been around the block a few times is that as teachers we must be aware of these differences and address them with our students. You know, make them aware that these gender biases are out there. I feel that by bringing awareness to the biases and stereotypes I am helping them to dispel them. It is my hope

Case 5

that someday soon we can see both genders on an equal playing field. Now, ladies if you will excuse me, I believe that bell is about to ring signaling that our students' young minds will need nurturing." They all wave goodbye as they each head toward their classrooms to begin their afternoon of classes.

DISCUSSION QUESTIONS

1. Gender Differences and Stereotypes
   a. Explain the difference between sex and gender. Why is this difference an important one?
   b. How are gender differences expressed socially in the classroom? Discuss what a gender stereotype is and what typical gender stereotypes are evident in this case. What problems are created by gender stereotypes?
   c. Discuss the meaning of a gender role. How do gender roles play a role in an adolescent's understanding of jobs and careers. What gender roles are expressed in this case? Were they traditional roles for each gender? Why or why not?
   d. Assess how the teacher's aide's comment of "boys will be boys" can be interpreted in regard to gender role development. How has the teacher's aide's own experiences helped to explain her position on gender?
   e. How can students' self-esteem and self-concept be affected by gender, especially if they challenge the traditional gender role or stereotype for their gender?
   f. Discuss how abiding by typical gender roles may affect both sexes negatively in the classroom. What pressures may exist for adolescents to adhere to traditional gender stereotypes?

2. Development and Socialization of Gender Roles
   a. How early are children taught information regarding gender? How do those early influences potentially shape children's conception of gender and affect their future behaviors and perceptions?
   b. In the case, it is clear that some students are adhering to traditional gender stereotypes both with regard to school subjects and in social aspects. Choose examples from the case that demonstrate this and determine whether the students are negatively affected by their beliefs or actions.
   c. What role does the "self-fulfilling prophecy" have in perpetuating gender roles and gender stereotypes? Do you see evidence that this could be a possible outcome in some of the students in this class? Why or why not?

d. Evaluate how parents, siblings, and teachers can be a major factor in socializing gender role behavior. What evidence was presented in this case that would support this claim?

e. Assess how a parent, sibling, peer, teacher, or tutor's behavior may inadvertently be accountable for imparting gender stereotypes. What evidence do you see of this in this classroom?

3. Equitable Teaching Practices
   a. Ascertain what evidence of gender bias against either gender is evident in this case. Is the teacher aware that it is occurring? Does the teacher address any and all gender stereotypes or biases that are occurring in her classroom?
   b. Discuss how gender bias can unintentionally occur in the classroom. What is the importance of acting in a way that diminishes gender biases in the classroom?
   c. Judge the comment that Lance offers about making students aware of the potential differences in their performance due to their gender. Do you believe that awareness can potentially help to dissipate the stereotype?
   d. How is the teacher attempting to accommodate the different genders in her teaching practices? How can you avoid sexism in your teaching?
   e. STEM (science, technology, engineering, and math) is mentioned in this case with regard to its incorporation both in the curriculum and in future careers for these students. Evaluate the importance of making female students understand the importance of these subjects early in their education.
   f. Lance suggests that Mrs. Mendez take a look at her assessments. What types of alternative assessments could this teacher employ to supplement the traditional paper and pencil exams?
   g. Lance discusses that gender inequality occurs for both females and males. Discuss the effects these inequalities may pose for students' belief in their own ability as well as future career paths.
   h. Debate the pros and cons of single-sex education. Is this really a viable alternative to facilitating both genders' learning? What ramifications can teaching the two sexes in isolation pose for higher learning and future career success?

Case 6

Teaching Students with Special Learning Challenges

Suggested Theories: Exceptional Student Education (ESE), Attention Deficit
   Hyperactivity Disorder (ADHD), Learning Disabilities, and Parent Involvement
Teacher Challenges: Identifying and Teaching Students with Disabilities
Student Level: Middle School

Manny Gonzalez is a new seventh-grade teacher at Newgate Middle School. The new school year is beginning, and he is looking over the records of his incoming language arts students. He notices he has one ESE student, identified as having ADHD. He has already noted key strategies proven to be effective in working with students with this challenge by reflecting on his own teacher preparation training as well as working closely with the students' Individual Education Plan (IEP) and associated staff at the school. He moves on to looking over his lesson plans for the first few weeks of school, making sure all is in order.

During the first week of his second-period class, his students are busily engaged in their cooperative learning groups completing a worksheet activity explaining how specific images, like diagrams of how a machine works, contribute to and clarify textual material. He is sitting at his desk catching up on some grading as he makes a visual sweep of the classroom. He notices that one group seems to be off task, so he decides to make his way back there. Randall, his student identified with ADHD, has become physically animated in an exchange with two of his group members. Mr. Gonzalez queries, "What seems to be the problem Randall?"

Randall takes a deep breath and through gritted teeth mumbles, "I really don't like this project, and they are taking way too long to finish. So I was just trying to speed things up!" Koko, one of Randall's group members, speaks up. "I'm sorry, Mr. Gonzalez, but Randall is making many careless mistakes

45

on our worksheet. And he isn't listening when one of us tries to point them out to him. He just interrupts us and tries to blurt out the first answer he thinks of!" Mr. Gonzalez attempts to smooth things over with the group by asking everyone to be patient and reminding Randall this is a group exercise and everyone must participate to receive credit.

The following day, the class is engaged in a silent seat-work activity. The teacher has set up various learning resources around the room, including centers on inspiring works in the literature, tips for working with informational text, and a poetry station. Some stations feature charts, visuals, and original works, and others utilize technology resources like computer slide presentations and helpful online resources. When students complete a given worksheet, they are allowed to get up and visit the accompanying learning center. Mr. Gonzalez designed this with Randall in mind but realized immediately that it would be engaging for all students.

The combination of opportunities to retain information multimodally as well as occasions to move about the room would be appreciated by all. He's also set up a conference with Randall's parents later next week to discuss strategies that may have been effective in the past with Randall. He also wants to establish a work routine journal so Randall can set up short-term goals for the longer class assignments that will be forthcoming later in the school year. Mr. Gonzalez has noticed that Randall is already having difficulty organizing his initial handouts and notes to begin an upcoming long-term project on his chosen literary figure's most notable works.

Mr. Gonzalez circles about the classroom and notices that one of his quieter students, Aaliyah, seems to be flustered as she works through the reading passage. He notes that Aaliyah has taken considerably more time to get through the sequence of reading assignments than the rest of the class. He leans down to her desk and asks, "How's it going, Aaliyah? I notice it is taking you a bit longer to get through these reading exercises. Can I help in anyway?"

Aaliyah sighs and responds in a very dejected fashion, "Not really. I am just not a very good reader. It doesn't really matter what I do; it takes me so much longer than everyone else. I have a real problem with the vocabulary, and I keep losing my place. I don't even know why I bother trying to get through this stuff. When you explain it in class, I understand so much better. Even the learning centers are more helpful." Mr. Gonzalez smiles in encouragement and points to the nearest learning center. "Why don't you go ahead and visit that learning center for now. We'll talk more about this later."

He wonders if it is possible that Aaliyah has a reading-specific learning disability because she usually responds very well in class, but her performance on various assignments and quizzes is surprisingly lower than to be expected. In particular, she has trouble with phonemic awareness, spelling, and questions on reading comprehension. Mr. Gonzalez decides to schedule a visit with Mrs. Goldberg, the ESE specialist, to discuss his concerns. As he checks on Randall, he also notes that while he is not getting into any trouble and is remaining in his seat, he is fidgeting by snapping his pencil repeatedly against his knee and mumbling what appears to be song lyrics, behavior that seems to be only a minor source of distraction to his closest neighbor.

Later, after school that day, Manny stops by to see Mrs. Goldberg and discuss his concerns about Aaliyah. He shares that while he understands the basics of ESE placement and services, he is so new to teaching that the subtleties of the process elude him. He wants to be sure he helps Aaliyah as much as he can, and he proceeds to share the symptoms he has identified in Aaliyah that might preclude a learning disability.

"Manny, you have done exactly the correct thing. This speaks well of your natural gut instincts in teaching," Mrs. Goldberg responds with a knowing smile. "Maybe it would help if I shared our school's policy in referring students for ESE placement. And, first things first. Have you contacted Aaliyah's parents? A referral for evaluation has to be the first step. You also need to check the student's cumulative file. Has she previously qualified for special services or been tested for possible placement? What about her general academic progress as well as within specific subject areas like math or reading?"

Manny is furiously scribbling down Mrs. Goldberg's suggestions and takes a deep breath before holding up his hands in an obvious sign of information overload. "Wait a minute. Slow down. I clearly haven't done any of these things and am just at the beginning of this process. I see I have a great deal to learn. And I haven't even had the chance to converse with you about Randall Thompson's IEP. I have tried a few things but was hoping to get more suggestions from you on adapting my instruction to his particular learning needs. I am particularly concerned about my upcoming unit assessment and any accommodations I should make for him. Any chance I can talk you into a cup of coffee or tea after we leave here today?"

Mrs. Goldberg checks her watch, realizing the obvious potential in this just-out-of-graduate-school candidate, and smiles warmly. "Of course, Manny, I am always available to teachers who are clearly willing to learn about the ways to meet all their students' learning needs. I don't want to overwhelm you, but I will begin to update you on another student who'll be in one of your later classes. He's new to the school and has a form of high-functioning autism. I would like to discuss with you some key ideas in terms of behavioral and learning expectations, his IEP goals and objectives, and positive behavioral support."

DISCUSSION QUESTIONS

1. ADHD
    a. Identify the typical symptoms associated with ADHD. Why would teachers' ability to identify the symptoms of ADD and ADHD in their students be of importance?
    b. Which symptoms of ADD or ADHD do you notice in Randall? What kinds of accommodations might Randall and other students who have ADHD need in the classroom?
    c. Discuss the challenges that students diagnosed with ADD or ADHD face with regard to academic success.
    d. Is ADD or ADHD a disorder that students typically outgrow before reaching adulthood? Does it worsen or lessen as students age or is this a common misconception?
    e. Discuss the research that exists with regard to students' various treatment options or diet choices that could assist them in battling ADD/ADHD.
    f. Analyze the advantages and problems associated with labeling students as ADD/ADHD.
    g. Aside from ADD/ADHD what other disabilities are prevalent in today's classroom? What about in the ages you plan to teach?

2. Learning Disabilities
    a. Identify the typical symptoms associated with learning disabilities. Which do you notice in Aaliyah's behavior? In particular, what reading-specific learning disability do you see potential evidence of in this case? What is phonemic awareness?
    b. Outline the typical process for referring students like Aaliyah to ESE services. What is a teacher's role in identifying students with a learning disability?
    c. Create a potential IEP for Aaliyah.
    d. Evaluate possible testing accommodations appropriate for students with a learning disability.

3. Learning and Instruction
    a. What can you do to encourage engaging instruction for all students?
    b. Discuss the effective utilization of learning centers in the middle school classroom. How can they best be organized to scaffold student learning given varying levels of academic performance and independent learning? How can learning centers be used to individualize instruction?
    c. What other constructivist teaching methods might be used to engage students in active and authentic learning as an alternative to learning centers?

d. What role might instructional technology play in your classroom? How important is multimodal learning for students' retention? How might technology be effectively used for teaching students with a learning disability?

4. Classroom Management
   a. Can you create some classroom management strategies that would work for Randall as well as the classroom more generally?
   b. How can teachers make changes in the classroom to help minimize the distractions and disruptions of ADHD? Discuss preventive strategies pertaining to seating, organization of classroom environment, delivery of instructions, and cueing.
   c. What cautions would you add that pertain to disciplining students with emotional or behavioral problems specifically?

5. Parent Involvement
   a. Identify parental rights in relation to referring students to ESE services.
   b. What suggestions might you present to Mr. Gonzalez as he prepares to contact Aaliyah's and Randall's parents?
   c. Evaluate how teachers can best communicate with parents and families as educational partners.
   d. Discuss sensitive and appropriate ways a teacher might suggest a child receive a referral for evaluation.

Part III

LEARNING THEORIES

Cell Phones in Class

Problems with Texting

Suggested Theories: Classical Conditioning, Classroom Management, and
Adolescent Social Development
Teacher Challenges: Cell Phone Distractions in the Classroom, Social Media
and Adolescent Development
Student Level: Middle School

The bell just rang at Pines Middle School indicating that students will have
five minutes to reach their next class of the day. Students are scattering about
trying to reach their lockers and switch books in time for their next class.
Emily and Samantha are seventh-grade students taking a moment to catch
up before they head to English class together. "Emily! Hey, wait up!" yells
Samantha. Emily, pleased to see her best friend coming her way, pauses to
allow for her friend to catch up to her.

"How was biology?" Samantha asks. "Pretty boring except that Noah swal-
lowed his gum so that Mr. Nguyen wouldn't give him a detention, and he
ended up choking in the process . . . it was pretty funny!" exclaims Emily. "I
bet!" says Samantha, and both girls laugh. As the girls approach their lockers Jordan, the boy Emily has a crush on, is standing nearby chatting with
friends. "Look, Emily, there he is . . . and I think he is looking this way!"
says Samantha excitedly. "I doubt it," Emily says, as she looks down at her
feet and then shifts her weight nervously. She then turns her head and quickly
opens her locker.

As Emily reaches for her English book, she notices Samantha is no longer
standing next to her. In fact, since Samantha already had the book she needed
for the next class in her bag, she did not stop by her locker. Instead, she
walked over to where Jordan was standing and is now talking to him. Emily
closes her locker and nervously waits for Samantha to return. As they walk

to their English literature and composition class, Samantha tells Emily that she has something to tell her, but they reach Mr. Robinson's classroom before they have a chance to discuss the conversation that Samantha had with Jordan.

Mr. Robinson has his students seated in rows that face the front of the class, with his desk situated in front. Fearing they'll be marked tardy because Mr. Robinson is stern with classroom rules, both girls head toward their assigned seats, with Samantha promising to send Emily a text. The late bell rings, and students rush to find their seats and begin work on the "problem of the day," a brain teaser on writing mechanics that Mr. Robinson presents on the board daily. Students are to work on it as he takes attendance. Emily is working on the problem of the day but is having trouble concentrating since she is anxiously awaiting Samantha's text.

As Emily finishes her answer to the problem, her phone's text notification goes off. It must be from Samantha, she thinks to herself. Ensuring that Mr. Robinson is not looking, Emily quickly takes the phone out and sets it to silent mode, which she forgot to do before class having been preoccupied with worrying about Samantha's talk with Jordan. She inwardly cringes, knowing the teacher has a strict policy on cell phones not being out in the classroom and that they should be kept stored away in students' backpacks. However, believing that Mr. Robinson is busy taking attendance, Emily opens the message and begins to read it.

Emily is so distracted that she doesn't realize Mr. Robinson is walking over to her seat. She suddenly hears a noise beside her seat, and much to her dismay discovers Mr. Robinson standing above her desk. Before Emily has a chance to put her phone away, Mr. Robinson takes it and heads to the front of the classroom. Emily stares in disbelief; she thinks she hears her friend say something, but Emily is not focusing on anything but Mr. Robinson. Mr. Robinson reaches his desk and turns to face the class. Emily grimly recognizes she's going to become the target of one of his more favored soap box speeches on cell phones being out during class.

"Well, class, I noticed that Emily chose not to be on task with answering the problem of the day, so I thought I would share what she felt was more important with the entire class by reading her text aloud." Emily is in a panic and attempts to stop him by saying, "No, Mr. Robinson, I apologize and will put my phone away if . . ." She trails off as Mr. Robinson does not acknowledge her response and instead acts as if he will proceed with reading the text aloud to the class.

Emily is very embarrassed because the text reveals she has feelings for Jordan and she'd like to go out with him. Many of the students in the class know Jordan; in fact, some are his basketball teammates. Fearing that she'll be unable to stop the tears from running down her face, Emily runs out of the room and goes to the girl's bathroom. She's mortified and can't imagine facing her classmates again. After all, right after class, Jordan will surely be informed of what happened, and she fears she'll be unable to face him as well. She wants to leave before the class ends; she calls home from the office and asks to be picked up because she isn't feeling well.

Later that night, Samantha calls Emily's home phone several times, but Emily just does not feel like talking and asks her mom to take a message. She only just realizes with further bleak resignation that her cell phone is still at school, left behind in English class.

The following day, Emily awakens when her alarm clock goes off. She begins to get ready for school like usual until she remembers the incidence in Mr. Robinson's class. Emily suddenly begins to feel ill—her stomach begins to hurt, and she begins to sweat. Emily tells her parents that she does not feel well and that she would like to stay home. Since Emily has not missed many school days, her parents agree. However, after Emily claims she is sick the following day, her parents warn her that if her condition does not improve she will have to visit the doctor.

Days later, when Emily returns to school, she decides to skip Mr. Robinson's class as well as another class that shares a lot of the same students from English. The thought of entering either class makes Emily feel ill, and in particular, thinking about being in the presence of Mr. Robinson makes her feel very ill. Emily has not returned to Mr. Robinson's class since the incident took place over a week ago, and Mr. Robinson has now asked to see her parents. And if that is not bad enough, Emily heard there are some rumors going around about her on social media. She feared that might be the case with how quickly information spreads.

She's avoided social media, especially since she still hasn't gotten her cell phone back. Samantha confirmed Emily's worst fears that she had indeed gone viral on some of the more well-known student Twitter accounts at the school. Apparently another girl overheard Samantha discussing what was occurring and leaked it in a text, which was forwarded to other students in the school. Emily is frustrated, angry, and embarrassed all at the same time. She just doesn't know what to do to best cope with all the fallout at school.

While Emily struggles with the social repercussions of what happened, across campus Mr. Robinson is sharing his take on what occurred with one of the other seventh-grade language arts teachers, Miley Denton. As they make their way to their next class, he shares with Miley, "I know I often criticize how much texting slang creeps into my students' writing, but my bigger teaching challenge is that cell phones in class are a constant distraction from instruction! This student was very upset when I enforced my rule and took her phone as she was using it in my class. I mentioned to the class only that the text was about the boy she liked. I didn't actually read the text itself—I would never do that!" Clearly frustrated, he continues, "However, she abruptly left class and went home. She was out of school the next day. Then, she skipped my class for a while, and I had to speak to her parents both to return the phone and to discuss the unexcused absences. I felt really bad because while I would never actually read a student's private text in class, I did want to make a point! Clearly, in retrospect, I could have handled this better. What do you do when faced with students disobeying you and using their cell phones?"

Miley looks on with empathy before saying, "I have also struggled with how to handle this given lack of a school-wide approach. I think the school needs to come up with a clearer policy on cell phone use in the classroom. For example, I know some teachers actually find creative ways to put these cell phones to work for learning purposes by having students use them to look up supporting research or outside sources. Perhaps we should bring this all up at the next department meeting. Maybe if we came up with something in the English department, we could take it to the principal for faculty-wide consideration."

DISCUSSION QUESTIONS

1. Classical Conditioning
   a. Compare classical conditioning to operant conditioning. What evidence do you see that demonstrates classical conditioning is taking place in this case?
   b. Diagram the unconditioned stimulus, the unconditioned response, the conditioned stimulus, and the conditioned response in this case.
   c. Decide whether a generalization has occurred. Support your answer with examples from the case.
   d. Explain how the conditioned response in this case may be extinguished.
   e. Outline how you would ensure that the type of classical conditioning demonstrated in this case does not happen in your classroom.
   f. Discuss some possible ramifications that this classical conditioning scenario can have in the future. Alternatively, can you think of any potential benefits that classical conditioning can have in classroom situations?

2. Cell Phones in the Classroom
   a. With regard to the text message, generate tactics for how to improve Mr. Robinson's behavior modification. Discuss how you would handle a similar incident involving students' use of cell phones in your classroom.
   b. Should cell phones be forbidden in class, for instance, by teachers asking students to check their phones in as they come to class? Or should teachers confiscate students' phones after violating classroom policies that phones stay out of sight?

c. Should teachers read students' text messages? What about the argument that teachers might be able to look through a student's phone to prevent instances of bullying or cyberbullying? However, at what point is it an invasion of privacy?

d. How might cell phones be used for beneficial instructional purposes? Should instructors put those cell phones to work by students using them for research and learning purposes in the classroom?

e. Mr. Robinson is a language arts teacher, but regardless of the subject being taught, how would you address texting slang being used in students' formal writing on class assignments? Does the use of texting and electronic messaging impact students' oral and written communication in the classroom?

3. Classroom Management
   a. Explain the type of behavior modification that is taking place in this case. How effective is it from a classroom management perspective?
   b. Explain whether you would classify Mr. Robinson's management strategy as a minor or a moderate intervention.
   c. Does Mr. Robinson demonstrate "withitness" in the classroom? If so, how? Is he effective?
   d. With regard to the physical makeup of the classroom, what type of arrangement style does Mr. Robinson have in his classroom? How is that evident in the case?
   e. Justify how Mr. Robinson uses the "problem of the day" with regard to classroom management. Judge its effectiveness as a management strategy.
   f. Share the implications that the theory of classical conditioning has on classroom management models.
   g. Discuss the importance of a nonthreatening environment and how teachers can provide stimuli that will elicit positive emotional responses.

4. Social Development
   a. How may Mr. Robinson's behavior affect Emily's self-esteem? Her self-concept?
   b. Discuss how Emily's peers and her friendship with Samantha play a role in her behavior. Summarize the effects of peer relations on teen behaviors.
   c. Judging from the case, can you determine Emily's peer status? Why or why not? How could peer status affect Emily's behavior?
   d. How does the rising use of social media affect teenagers' development of social skills and quality of social relationships?
   e. How has cell phone texting, a preferred mode of adolescent communication, impacted teens' social development? How does texting impact

adolescents' face-to-face communication skills as well as contribute to instances of teasing or bullying?

f. For some, texting has become almost a compulsion. How does compulsive texting affect adolescents' academic learning? Social development?

Case 8

Adolescent Relationships and the Power of Social Media

Suggested Theories: Social Cognitive Theory, Observational Learning, Modeling, Cognitive Development, and Personality Development
Teacher Challenges: Social Media, Peer Acceptance, and Social Well-Being in Adolescence
Student Level: High School

Maggie Moreno and Navya Patel are both ninth-grade teachers at Central High School; Maggie teaches English and Navya teaches math. The two know each other well, as they attended the same university where they earned their bachelor's degrees in education. The two greet each other happily and enter the school for tonight's pep rally and basketball game. The teachers follow the colorful banners decorating the hallways announcing the various student council events, and many are for the student-council elections, which will be held next week.

The teachers discuss how several of their students are running for student council this year and they are excited to see who will win the coveted leadership roles. Seeing a group of their students at the student council tables selling various snacks and drinks, both teachers head in that direction. "Hi, ladies," Mrs. Moreno says in a friendly manner, and all the students greet her and Mrs. Patel happily. "Hi, Mrs. Moreno. Can I get you anything?" Jayla, a ninth-grader in Mrs. Moreno's third period, asks as she and the other students help the teachers with their orders.

Jayla is normally a little shy but always has a joyful demeanor; however, tonight Mrs. Moreno thinks that she doesn't seem to be acting like herself and wonders if something is wrong. She decides against asking her since they are in a crowded gymnasium. "Don't forget about the quiz tomorrow, Jayla!" Mrs. Moreno says as the teachers walk toward the bleachers to find a seat. As the teachers walk off, two of the students begin to talk. "You are going to have to do better than that if you don't want the teachers to start asking you questions," Brooklyn, Jayla's best friend, says in a hushed voice next to Jayla. "Ah, really? Is it that obvious?" Jayla asks nervously.

"Well, yeah . . . you totally look a mess. I mean I get it though. Why don't you go to the bathroom and either take off your eye makeup or fix it so you can't see you've been crying. I'll cover for you," Brooklyn says sympathetically. Jayla grabs her purse and heads in the direction of the restroom. Jayla still cannot believe that Price, her now ex-boyfriend, acted so heartlessly. She never thought he'd be so callous as to end their relationship in a text and then block her number as well as unfriend her on social media. She knew people did that, but she thought Price was different—she'd known him since they were in elementary school.

Dealing with all this has made her forget about her schoolwork, and now Mrs. Moreno mentioned a quiz that she forgot to study for! Oh, and seeing another one of her teachers reminded her that she had not completed the chapter summaries for his class, nor had she read over the material for Mrs. Patel's homework quiz. She can't seem to remember the due date! And she has a science vocabulary test tomorrow, or is it the next day? She thinks, *this isn't like me; I am a very good student!* As Jayla exits the bathroom she is flustered and isn't watching where she is going. She almost collides with a group of students who are standing by the bathroom.

"Sorry, excuse me!" Jayla shouts over the game but freezes when she sees Price standing with them. She can hear snickering coming from the group and realizes that Price has his arm around another girl's shoulder. Jayla feels as if she is going to be sick. Brooklyn pulls on her hand and gets her back behind the student council table. "Jayla, I wasn't going to show you, but it looks like you just found out. It's all over social media that Price is dating someone new." Brooklyn shares her phone screen with Jayla to show her the recent post. Jayla cannot understand what is happening. She didn't do anything wrong; they didn't even have a fight!

Maggie Moreno sees the interchange between Jayla and her friend from her seat high above the court in the bleachers where she is seated with other ninth-grade teachers. Due to their school's team teaching protocols, they all know each other well. "Anyone notice something going on with Jayla?" Maggie asks. "Oh, you didn't hear? Seems she and her boyfriend broke up. From what I hear, he was heartless sending her a quick text and turning to social media to spread the word. He unfriended her on social media and so did his friends. So expect some extra drama in your classes this week," replies Bruno Melendez, a social studies teacher.

Maggie knew Jayla was acting different tonight! However, she had not met with her third-period class today because of a school assembly, which is the class that both Jayla and her boyfriend Price are in. Maggie is immediately overcome with feelings of empathy for Jayla, as she knows how social relationships, romantic or otherwise, rule students' lives. Xavier Hawkins, a science teacher, shakes his head in disbelief and says, "I'm stunned. I know Price both from class and ecology club. I didn't think him capable of this kind of meanness. He's outgoing and enjoys female attention, but he's also kindhearted and has an easygoing temperament."

All of the other teachers agree. Navya responds, "I have Price in my early engineers club and on the math team, and I too did not expect this! But I was a bit shocked when I saw some of my students' online profiles. My babysitter is friends with many of my students, and I saw a definite disconnect between the students we know in class and how they make themselves appear online. It's clear their looks and actions are influenced by what they observe actors, athletes, singers, and others doing on their social media accounts. I now see how they bring those online perceptions or stereotypes into the classroom discussions."

Maggie sighs and adds, "And the problem is that because our students spend so much time interacting online via texts or instant messages, they miss out on seeing a person's body language or the effect their words are having emotionally on another person. I think that's why they find it easier to be cruel to someone via a text or online than they would if they were face-to-face."

Bruno takes a sip of his soda and says, "Absolutely! I just had a problem with two of my students who get along great in real time but are always fighting online. When they sat with me for detention one afternoon, I discovered that they fight over one not liking the other's pictures enough or one girl not including the other girl in her comments or pictures. Ultimately it seems to me that social media is conducive to coaching our young students into disagreeing and fighting in ways that endanger their friendships."

Xavier emphatically agrees, "Yes! And making the situation worse is the number of likes their pictures, videos, and comments instantly receive since they spend so much time on their phones. They are constantly engaged in a popularity contest and feeling pressure to fit in," Xavier points to his phone, "by continuously posting where they are, what they ate, what they bought, and who they're with. Like in this case, with Jayla and Price, he posts pictures with another girl, and even some of Jayla's friends, who should be loyal to her and disapprove of his hurting their friend, I heard liked it, thus rewarding him for his insensitive and negative behavior. This can easily add to a student's sense of isolation and betrayal as well as lead to depression." All of them nod in agreement.

Later in the week, Mrs. Moreno asks to meet with the students who did not pass the last major assignment. She wants to determine whether she can help them succeed and suggest better study strategies. Her students share that they don't feel they have time to do many of the worksheets and practice test questions she posts on the class's website. While some of the reasons they offer is other class work, some signal to a problem with time management because they get constantly distracted by what is going on with their friends.

When she asks them if their parents are disturbed by late-night phone calls, they answer that they silence their phones and computers and communicate via text, social media, or instant messaging. This sleep deprivation certainly explains why she sees many of them attempting to complete work in the courtyard before school, which is not going to help them in learning or reviewing the concepts, and why the first period of the day is very difficult to engage the students in class discussions.

Mrs. Moreno addresses another concern. "Many of your papers," she says to her class, "when handwritten resemble the lingo you must be using online. I can't understand any of it! You are using abbreviations that aren't proper grammar. It is text slang." Many of the students apologize but say they're not worried about learning grammar because they expect to always use word processing programs that correct their grammar. Similarly, they tell her they don't believe in having to commit information to memory or retain information because they rely on the accessibility of information on the Internet to give them the knowledge they seek.

Jayla decides to wait for all her classmates to leave before approaching Mrs. Moreno. Jayla has always liked Mrs. Moreno because she feels that she's strict but fair and always willing to listen to students. "Mrs. Moreno, can I speak with you?" Jayla asks shyly while standing by the side of her teacher's desk. "Sure!" Mrs. Moreno replies, and the two of them begin to chat. Since it is Mrs. Moreno's planning period, Jayla feels that she can talk a bit longer about what has been going on, and Mrs. Moreno reassures her by saying, "Don't worry, Jayla, I'll give you a pass to your next class. Now, what was the problem today that caused your group not to get the work done?"

Jayla looks down at the chair that Mrs. Moreno offers and takes a seat. "Well, I'm sure you heard . . . everyone has . . . about me and Price . . . it's hard because we have many of the same classes, you know? He isn't like he acts, especially not the way he does online, but . . . well, his friends tell him that's what cool athletes do—have tons of girlfriends and earn millions playing sports. It's a mess because some of my friends still like him and follow him on social media. It's awkward when they tell me. My group today had a few of his friends in it, and we all could not get along, and of course we didn't finish the assignment. I'm so sorry about all this!"

Maggie thinks about today's class, and Jayla's description was indeed accurate since the students had been rowdier than usual, constantly whispering and trying covertly to sneak peeks at their phones. It was obvious that the class had divided itself into two social camps: Price's friends and Jayla's.

Since it affected students' class participation, she began handing out warnings, and those who already had earned a warning in her class were given an after-school detention. Watching some students get punished certainly deterred others from engaging in negative behavior.

Mrs. Moreno smiles sympathetically saying, "Jayla, there's no need to apologize for what's happening in my class or any other class, as you are not at fault. You have always been an excellent student, and I don't want to see you change that. I'm certain this breakup hasn't been easy since you share classes and friends and it appears many of your friends are modeling unkind behavior and encouraging others to do the same. I will certainly do all I can to help you catch up, and I urge you to speak to your other teachers as well if your work has been affected. I also would ask that you please consider seeing the school counselor."

DISCUSSION QUESTIONS

1. Social Cognitive Theory and Observational Learning
   a. Describe how elements of Bandura's social cognitive theory are taking place in this case.
   b. Identify examples of observational learning that are taking place in this case. What role might observational learning play in creating students' clique-like behavior?
   c. What role does social reinforcement such as likes in social media play in clique-like behavior? How does social media reinforce group boundaries and assist in the development and perpetuating of negative behaviors?
   d. What role does television, sports, and the music industry play in the potential for broader social modeling to explain adolescent behaviors? How can teachers expose students to positive symbolic models or be positive role models themselves?
   e. Discuss the problems that Maggie Moreno is encountering regarding achieving successful cooperative learning in her classroom? How can she use heterogeneous grouping to help students appreciate individual differences?
   f. Outline examples from the case in which the students are learning via inhibition/disinhibition and/or response facilitation.
   g. Explain examples of vicarious reinforcement and vicarious punishment that take place in this case. How have they been affected by online presence?
   h. What is self-regulated learning, and which event in the case do you see this relate to? How can students' academic behaviors be affected

by lack of sleep and constant social pressures to fit in with the group
as well as to present themselves online in a way that others approve?

2. Effects of Social Media
   a. What overall teaching challenges are the teachers discussing that seem
      to be occurring as a result of social media? What strategies can you
      devise that could assist them?
   b. How is social media assisting students in engaging in and learning
      negative behaviors? What dangers does this pose for adolescent bully-
      ing, depression, or withdrawal?
   c. Reflect on the positions that the teachers are taking regarding students'
      online representations of themselves. Discuss the risks that teachers
      and parents should be aware of regarding young adolescents creating
      personalities based on social media.
   d. Discuss the challenges that communicating via online methods pose
      for adolescents' development of appropriate prosocial skills and the
      emotional values such as empathy.
   e. Outline the concerns that Maggie finds in her classroom regarding
      online communications affecting students' grammatical writing. What
      is text slang? What complications does this create with regard to future
      grammatical challenges?
   f. Evaluate the challenges that teachers face regarding student engage-
      ment in the classroom when having to compete with adolescents' sleep
      deprivation and social media.

3. Cognitive Development in Adolescence
   a. According to Piaget, identify the stage of cognitive development stu-
      dents are likely to be in.
   b. What role does idealistic thinking play in adolescents' cognitive
      development, and how can teachers help students to face realistic
      challenges?
   c. What role might adolescent egocentrism play in the decision making
      and behaviors that the students are exhibiting online and toward each
      other?
   d. How can social media's ability to spread a rumor instantly or to give
      instant gratification from earning likes on adolescents' social media
      posts impact adolescent egocentrism? What effects would this pose for
      the classroom?
   e. Discuss brain development during adolescence. How does ongoing
      development in the prefrontal cortex influence adolescents' decision
      making and judgment during stressful situations?

f. Outline the hazards that sleep deprivation can have on a developing brain as well as impairments that could occur as a result of long-term exposure.

g. Discuss strategies or tactics in which teachers can assist students in reducing their adolescent egocentrism.

h. Discuss the role that social media plays in adolescents' cognitive development. How may it impede, rather than assist, adolescents' cognitive growth?

4. Erikson's Theory of Personality Development and Identity

a. Discuss which stage of Erikson's theory these students are likely to be in. How are the events of the case affecting students' development of identity?

b. The teachers discuss believing that their students are presenting themselves online differently than they are in person. Discuss the risks young adolescents face in keeping up two different versions of themselves. What dangers can exist when they need to balance or bridge both of those versions of themselves?

c. How can teachers assist their students' development of identity? How can students like Jayla have trouble with their identity and self-esteem due to the circumstances of a breakup?

d. Determine how teachers could use Marcia's identity development to better understand where each of the students is with respect to his or her identity status. Discuss how each of the classifications of Marcia's identity statuses describe how a person's identity forms.

e. Explain the role that social media plays in adolescents' development of personality. How may it impede and hinder adolescents' quest for identity development?

Case 9

Grade Grubbing

Complaining and Arguing about Grades

Suggested Theories: Learning Strategies, Metacognition, Self-Regulation, and
  Parent Involvement
Teacher Challenges: Students with Ineffective Study Skills, Engaging
  Disinterested Students, Handling Grade Complaints, and Demanding or
  Defensive Parents
Student Level: Middle School

Marilyn Gray is an eighth-grade student at Washington Middle School.
She and her friends are walking to their second-period classes. Marilyn's is
history and government with Ms. Williams, and upon seeing Ms. Williams
standing by the door, Marilyn inwardly groans because she realizes that she
once again forgot to bring in her makeup assignment—now way overdue.
Marilyn knows her teacher will ask for it after class because Ms. Williams is
super organized and never forgets anything.

The class gets started, and Ms. Williams passes back yesterday's quiz—
Marilyn cannot believe her eyes! Another bad grade? She didn't think this
quiz had been all that difficult. *Sure, I wasn't able to answer some of the
questions, but that couldn't have counted for that much, could it? What was
it Ms. Williams had said about studying for those? And how much did each
question count?* She can't remember the specifics although she knows the
teacher discussed it. *Guess I must have been daydreaming as I often find
myself doing in this class. Ms. Williams is just such a hard grader!* Marilyn
is feeling very stressed.

Marilyn continues thinking, *why is it that studying for this class doesn't
seem to get me anywhere? Why is it some of my friends coast by on hardly any
studying or effort yet still get good grades in this class? Everyone knows Ms.
Williams is a good teacher, so then why am I not just automatically learning?*

Marilyn sighs when she realizes she's missed the entire review for the quiz and that today's lesson has started.

After class, Ms. Williams motions for Marilyn to come to the far corner of the room, which is out of earshot of the students exiting the class. "Marilyn, your makeup assignment was due last week, and that was with the extra two-day extension. Did you bring it today?" Marilyn appears slightly put out and says, "I know. I forgot it at home, but I did it, I swear! I totally just forgot to bring it in! Sorry . . . I have had so much other work to do and . . . with having been sick I had so much work to make up . . . and your class is much harder than others . . . and well with cheerleading . . . I just keep forgetting."

Ms. Williams doesn't look convinced as she folds her arms in front of her and says, "Marilyn, you were ill three weeks ago for a few days; I have since given you more than sufficient time to make up all the assignments. In fact, at the request of your mother I gave you two more days on this assignment, and you have yet to turn it in—even with a late penalty."

"I know . . . I just forgot again. But, well, can't you just give me a passing score on it, or count the last assignment twice? I mean that's fair, right?" Marilyn asks her teacher. While Marilyn hasn't had any teacher really agree to this, she figures she'll keep trying. Maybe it will just work.

Ms. Williams cannot believe that once again Marilyn is using excuses for missing work or that she is complaining that the work is too hard. Marilyn habitually complains to her about being a hard grader when she does poorly on assignments, or that assignments weren't clearly explained, or that she wasn't given enough time. If not, she will tell her that she had too much to study for in other classes the night before. When Ms. Williams tells her how long she's had for the assignment or directs her to the class webpage where the directions for that assignment were posted, Marilyn usually says she forgot to look or she was confused.

Ms. Williams replies to Marilyn in a stern voice, "No, Marilyn, I cannot do that. You need to earn the grade like all the other students. I have given you more than enough time, and I have reminded you countless times, including yesterday when I saw you in the hall after your sixth-period class. Please have it in tomorrow if you do not want to earn a zero. Your grades in the class are poor, Marilyn, and I am concerned about your performance."

Marilyn says in a dejected tone, "I know, and I kept reminding myself as I walked to my locker yesterday. But then I don't know what happened; I just forgot. Believe me, I get it; I'll write it down on my planner again."

Marilyn arrives in her third-period class just before the bell rings. Making her way to her desk, she says hi to friends. Upon reaching her desk she tosses her backpack on the floor and slumps into her chair. Marilyn knows the conversation with Ms. Williams isn't over because from what she said, Marilyn isn't doing well. Plus, she knows that she isn't going to be able to turn in the makeup assignment tomorrow like she told Ms. Williams. Truth is, she wasn't honest with Ms. Williams when she told her she'd completed the assignment.

If Marilyn remembers correctly she's only gotten a couple of the questions done on the twenty-question assignment, and since she hasn't done any of the reading for the assignment it is unlikely she will be able to finish it by tomorrow. Marilyn has never been great at keeping track of her performance in Ms. Williams's class or other classes she doesn't enjoy or find interesting—she tends to leave studying or completing work for those classes for last and then falls behind. However, ever since her mom got a promotion at work that has her working late, she has not been home to regularly ask for her graded work, and things have gotten worse.

The next day in Ms. Williams's class, she has drawn these large bubbles on the whiteboard, and she has various government concepts in them that are part of today's lesson. Ms. Williams is explaining to the class how these concepts are all related and that the bubbles are a learning strategy called concept mapping that some may be familiar with. Ms. Williams then directs the class to several other examples of concept maps that she has put on display at the back of the class and instructs her students to create concept maps for tonight's homework much like they will be doing in class today.

Ms. Williams says she thinks this strategy will be beneficial since after reviewing previous coursework and assignments, she feels that some students are having difficulty organizing material and understanding higher order relationships. Concept maps, she says, will help students organize material and make associations between facts and ideas, making lessons easier to remember. Ms. Williams starts calling on students, and together the class is on their way to constructing the concept map together.

Marilyn is thankful to be sitting in the back. As she looks around the class, she sees the majority of the class participating, clearly following along with the strategy and evidently understanding the lesson. Ugh! Marilyn silently grumbles as she puts her head down on her desk and tunes out Ms. Williams. She mentally berates herself because she really shouldn't have skipped last night's reading . . . perhaps she wouldn't be so lost right now. I mean how can she be expected to create that concept map thingy if she had no clue what the concepts meant!

If Ms. Williams wasn't going to tell them exactly what she wanted them to put in each of the bubbles and how each bubble connected to the others, then she was not going to get it. Did Ms. Williams really think they were supposed to do this on their own? Marilyn thinks back to last night; she went into her room genuinely meaning to read for this class, but then she saw her playlist open on her computer and couldn't resist unwinding with a little music. Shortly after, when she was just about ready to start reading, she saw her sister come home, and she just had to go hear about her day—her sister is in high school, and Marilyn loves to hear all about what goes on.

Marilyn had finally gotten back to reading when she saw her kitten play-ing, and she couldn't resist taking videos of her to post on social media—her friends loved to see her kitten videos. Then, after dinner she told herself she needed to read for this class, but her phone reminder went off alerting her that her favorite television show was about to start. She could have opted to record the show and watch it at a later time, but that would have meant missing out on talking about the show with her friends today. *If only her mom hadn't got-ten that stupid promotion at her job that requires her to get home late every day*, Marilyn laments to herself.

Marilyn has always relied on her mom to keep her on track. Her mom is very involved in her life, always checking her graded assignments and telling her precisely how to improve. She'll talk to her teachers when she doesn't agree with a grade, which happens often, and helps her get started with take-home projects. Her mom will bring home all the materials she needs and check it when she's finished. If she meets the goals that her mother sets for her, then she will get extra rewards—like additional allowance money, new clothes, skipping chores, and so on. I mean how else is Marilyn supposed to have time for a social life if her mother doesn't help her!

After the lesson is finished, Ms. Williams instructs the students to sit in their assigned project groups to work on the quarter-long project. Marilyn's group's topic is balancing power between the states and the federal govern-ment, and the groups have been diligently working since the project is worth a large portion of their grade. "Now remember, class," Ms. Williams says pointing to the project's instructions projected onto the whiteboard from her computer screen and waiting to continue until all students are paying atten-tion, "as you know, you all were tasked with planning the project, managing the project, and monitoring your progress on the project. Because we are still in our early stages I do not expect that you have gotten very far, but at the end of the week remember that your project update sheet is due to me again. All of the students will complete their share of where exactly you all are with your work. Remember I need specifics, not just vague summaries." Marilyn cringes inwardly because she's just realized she hasn't started on her portion of the group assignment; however, judging by the materials on her classmates' desks, they all have.

As Marilyn looks to see just how little she's completed, Aria, one of the students in her group, startles her when she exclaims in alarm, "Marilyn! Where's your project folder? Tell me you didn't forget it again!" Marilyn looks down to see she's brought the wrong folder to class. Embarrassed, Marilyn says, "Sorry, they're the same color. I grabbed the wrong one." Lync, another group member, shakes his head in disbelief and says, "Seriously, Marilyn, you've got to commit to this work; we'll get a low grade on the group part if you don't do your part." All the group members nod in agree-ment, and knowing they're right, she promises she will try to do better.

Ms. Williams is circulating among the groups as is her common practice. Marilyn does not want Ms. Williams to see she's forgotten the project folder, so she tries to act busy reading in her textbook when she sees Ms. Williams come near—thank goodness Ms. Williams can't read her thoughts. Marilyn knows that if she looks like she's doing her work most teachers will just pass by. Ms. Williams stops to help the group beside Marilyn's, and the students all turn to hear laughing coming from the group.

It seems that one of her classmates was asking Ms. Williams a question about the assignment and realized that he had confused the information on this assignment with information about another class—one that has a project similar to this one but that they are much further along on. Ms. Williams explains to her students that this is a common mistake where information you have already learned can interfere with information you are learning while other times it is the other way around—new information gets in the way of being able to remember the information that is already in your brain.

"Holy cow!" says Nick, a student in the group that Ms. Williams is chatting with, "that is exactly what happened to me in algebra today! The last chapter's information kept creeping up in my mind and confusing me when I was taking the test today—guess it's because the old stuff was like the new stuff we're learning!" Ms. Williams agrees and the group continues to talk before Ms. Williams walks over to assist another group.

After school that day, Marilyn is heading toward cheerleading practice. Aria is also on the team and the girls converse in the locker room. "Hey, Marilyn, don't forget the history and government assignment tonight, OK? You want me to text you to remind you?" Aria asks hesitantly as if not wanting to upset Marilyn. "Yeah, would you?" Marilyn responds appearing unbothered at her friend's request. Aria nods and replies, "I was thinking . . . how come you never forget cheerleading practices even when days get changed or forget your work in the classes that you like, but you seem to be a mess with a class like history and government?"

Marilyn ponders that for a moment thinking her teammate is right. She replies, "Good question . . . guess it's because I'm good at remembering what I love and the other stuff is just not important to me so I forget it easier." As the girls reach the other cheerleaders on the field and begin their stretches, they discuss today's Spanish test that many of them took. Aubrey, the cheerleading captain, says she's pretty sure she did really well because this test required they learn the material in order, so she created silly images to help her remember.

"Like for example one of my vocabulary words was carta, which means letter in Spanish, so I imagined a letter in a cart. Another vocabulary word was amor, meaning love, so I imagined a suit of armor with a heart on it and it helped me remember!" Aubrey finishes.

"That's genius, though I can't ever do it. I end up spending more time trying to remember how to use the trick than on the information I'm supposed to be remembering. I stick to just reading and rereading the information over and over again until it hopefully sticks in my brain long enough for me to get to the test," Marilyn says and many of the other cheerleaders agree.

"C'mon. It's not that difficult. How about trying this one?" Aubrey insists, standing up and wiping the grass blades off her practice uniform. "Say, for example, that you want to remember the directions going clockwise north, east, south, west. Well, you can just make up a silly phrase that begins with the letter of each word like Never Eat Stinky Wasabi!" All the girls laugh in agreement that Aubrey's memory tricks are great; many discuss utilizing them in the future.

Later in the week, Marilyn is seated in Ms. Williams's class listening as the teacher starts the class off with a flow chart projected on the whiteboard with colorful boxes that flow from one to the other. She tells the class she's going to fill these boxes with information that students give her as they recall last night's reading, and she encourages them to share information from their lives that is relevant to the lesson—the Bill of Rights. Ms. Williams starts with the First Amendment, and students add information. Some students, like Lync, who have been to Washington, DC, are also adding personal anecdotes and information that relate to the lesson.

At the end of class, Ms. Williams hands back all of last week's graded work and tells them to see her if they have any questions. Marilyn sees she once again has earned low scores on most of the work—especially the most recent test! She makes her mind up to speak to the teacher again because she's sure Ms. Williams is going to ask for a meeting with her mom. Additionally, these grades surely brought down her grade point average, and she will likely be suspended from being able to cheer in the next few games. Marilyn is so frustrated! This is all Ms. Williams's fault! She arranges at the end of class to speak to Ms. Williams, and Ms. Williams agrees she'll meet her today after school.

During Ms. Williams's planning time, she calls and leaves a message for Marilyn's mom. Marilyn's mom tends to leave a series of voice mails, e-mail messages, or messages with the school secretaries when she is unhappy with Marilyn's grade. She always insists on challenging her grading practices, claiming she grades her daughter too harshly or that she is unreasonable in her expectations for assignments. She never wants her daughter to be penalized for missing or incomplete work, and she expects that Marilyn should be given more time, as she is only a child.

Her last e-mail was to inform Ms. Williams that she will be challenging the cheerleading coach's decision to suspend her daughter from cheering at the next few upcoming games. Ms. Williams hopes that Marilyn comes to meet with her this afternoon ready to listen to her suggestions on how she can improve. It is clear to her in her discussions with Marilyn that while she believes Marilyn is studying a long time, she is devoting only a small fraction of that time to learning the information and that most of the time, Marilyn is waiting until the last minute to study and cramming the night before the test.

She hopes to convey some helpful metacognitive strategies to Marilyn and wonders whether that might be helpful to review with others in the class. One of her students has an identified learning disability and struggles with storing and remembering information. This is one of the reasons she has made such an attempt to include concept mapping and other visual organizers in class activities although she knows it will benefit all of her students.

After school that day Marilyn came to meet with Ms. Williams, and while she appeared to still be irritated with Ms. Williams, she seemed to want to improve her grades as well as lift the suspension from the cheerleading squad. As they talk, Marilyn shares her study habits with Ms. Williams to which Ms. Williams responds, "I think you need to start by having a quiet space to work free of distractions. Also, start studying days in advance using the tips I gave your class in the study guide. You also need to start using the strategies that I teach in class other than just reading your notes—you have to change a strategy if it's proving ineffective, OK? Are you understanding what you are reading and learning? Do you monitor how your learning is going?"

Marilyn answers no to both questions, and it is clear to Ms. Williams why the student is failing. Ms. Williams concludes the meeting by offering Marilyn suggestions for time management, ideas on how she can assess her own progress as she reads the lessons, and to pair Marilyn with a classmate who excels in the class. Ms. Williams has chosen Lync because he's always demonstrated higher order thinking and an excellent grasp of the material in class; he's one of the highest performers.

Marilyn was excited at the idea, and Lync had agreed when Ms. Williams suggested offering him some extra credit for his help. Peer tutors have always worked well for her in the past for all the students involved. She hopes that Marilyn will take her suggestions seriously, and if so, then she looks forward to seeing her improve.

DISCUSSION QUESTIONS

1. Information Processing and Memory
   a. Discuss from the perspective of cognitive theory Marilyn's comment that if she appears busy her teacher cannot possibly read her thoughts.

What strategies can teachers employ that can assist in identifying whether students are off task?

b. Encoding, storing, and retrieval are important aspects of information processing. Discuss how Marilyn is demonstrating retrieval problems with being able to recall the teacher's directions or explanations that are linked to how she is encoding and subsequently storing. Generate ideas as to what the causes of Marilyn's problems with retrieval are.

c. Outline examples of how attention plays a role in memory. What problems is Marilyn having in this case with paying attention to her schoolwork? What is likely the cause of her attention problems? How could her disinterest in Ms. Williams's class influence her paying attention?

d. What struggles is Marilyn showing in short-term/working memory in Ms. Williams's class? From the perspective of memory, what is likely the reason that Marilyn is encountering those difficulties?

e. Marilyn struggles with remembering homework; however, why is Marilyn not having trouble remembering cheerleading practices? Why has she thought to set reminders on her phone when her favorite television program is on but is struggling to remember school assignments?

f. What short-term/working memory strategies can you identify were used by students in this case? Were the students successful in their remembering of the information when using the strategy? Why or why not?

g. What examples occur in the case that signal students are retrieving information stored in their long-term memory? Explain the example and how you would know that it is long-term memory.

h. Explain how a student in the case is demonstrating forgetting material due to interference. How can teachers assist students to forget less?

i. Everyone experiences what it is like to forget something. However, evaluate the differences between forgetting and laziness. Which is Marilyn displaying? Explain your answer.

2. Learning Strategies

a. How does a strategy like concept mapping aid our retrieval of information? What are some challenges that students like Marilyn might face with this strategy who are falling behind on the reading and therefore do not possess sufficient knowledge?

b. Elaborations aid our memory; summarize how elaborations are used in this case. What are some challenges that students may encounter with elaborations that would impede their using them successfully?

c. Identify mnemonics demonstrated in this case. What is the advantage of using mnemonics? What might Marilyn be struggling with when she says she can't seem to perform the strategy?

d. How can teachers assist students in being able to apply the mnemonics more effectively? How can using peer models and having student-generated examples help students to construct and use mnemonics?
e. Ms. Williams presents information in an organized manner; how does organization aid our memory? Generate other types of organization strategies that you could use in the classroom to aid your students' learning and recall of material.
f. Discuss how teachers' use of visual imagery can assist students' learning and recall of information. What other examples of visual imagery can teachers employ in the classroom?
g. In general, how can students' dislike of a school subject, such as Marilyn demonstrates with history and government, add to their lack of being able to employ successful learning strategies?

3. Metacognition
   a. What is metacognition? When do students typically develop metacognitive knowledge? What are the developmental trends in demonstrating these types of skills?
   b. Is Marilyn demonstrating that she possesses metacognition about her studies? Why or why not? Why is having metacognitive awareness important for students' learning?
   c. Based on what is presented in the case study, speculate about why Marilyn is struggling with metacognitive awareness. Is Marilyn attempting to understand why she is not doing well in Ms. Williams's class?
   d. Discuss how Marilyn doesn't seem to be performing poorly across all her courses and activities. Speculate about how Marilyn's priorities are likely influencing her success in Ms. Williams's class.
   e. What are effective learning and monitoring strategies this teacher might suggest for Marilyn? How can Ms. Williams support Marilyn in getting started?
   f. What are different ways teachers can encourage students' study skills and create ways to motivate and encourage success?
   g. Discuss how having a learning disability will interfere with students' metacognitive awareness. How can teachers prepare themselves with strategies and suggestions to assist these students to be successful?
   h. Outline how teachers should be vigilant about identifying students in their classes who are demonstrating a learning disability. From the information in this case, why is it likely that Marilyn's problems in Ms. Williams's class are not due to her having a learning disability? Use examples to demonstrate how this is so.

4. Self-Regulated Learning
   a. Explain what self-regulated learning is and how it is important for educational success.
   b. How is it shown in this case that Marilyn does not possess self-regulated learning in Ms. Williams's class? Use examples to demonstrate how this is so.
   c. Specifically, planning and monitoring are key in self-regulation. Demonstrate how Marilyn is struggling with planning for her schoolwork so that she has an organized way of approaching her studying and how she is not monitoring comprehension or revising strategies that aren't proving effective. How is the lack of effective planning and monitoring affecting her performance?
   d. Discuss how Marilyn is unable to self-monitor both her attention in Ms. Williams's class and at home when she is studying or how she is unable to self-monitor her performance in class. What examples from the case can you use to substantiate these points?
   e. Discuss the self-reflection component to self-regulation and how it impacts students' learning. Do you feel Marilyn has an internal or external attribution for her performance in Ms. Williams's class? How might teachers encourage students like Marilyn to reflect on their performance and adapt their strategies so they are more effective?
   f. What self-regulated learning advice can Ms. Williams share with Marilyn to improve her being able to self-regulate and improve her grades?
   g. What role do you see Marilyn's mom playing in her daughter's struggles with self-regulation?
   h. Students with disabilities often struggle with comprehension monitoring and rely on others' assistance to regulate their learning. Discuss the importance of teachers' being able to identify students who have learning disabilities and speculate on how teachers can provide assistance to students with learning disabilities so they may self-regulate successfully.
   i. Discuss why Marilyn's failure to self-regulate as demonstrated in the case study is not likely to be a result of a learning disability. What evidence in the case study supports this claim?

5. Parent and Student Complaints
   a. How can teachers most effectively handle students with chronic complaints about grades?
   b. Judge Ms. Williams's decision to stick to her rules and not allow Marilyn to turn in missing assignments or make up work past its due date as well as to not give her different opportunities than her other students received.
   c. How can overinvolved parents reinforce students' negative learning skills?

d. Discuss ideas for working with overinvolved parents or parents who are not likely to believe their students are at fault.
e. What school-wide resources or support may be helpful in assisting teachers to effectively handle challenging parents?

Part IV

MOTIVATION

Case 10

Encouraging Confidence in Math

Suggested Theories: Self-Efficacy, Learned Helplessness, Achievement Goals and Mindset, Attributional Theory, and Assessment
Teacher Challenges: Girls' Confidence in Math, Math Anxiety, Student Motivation and Engagement, Choosing Appropriate Assessment, Communication with Parents, and Student Disruptions
Student Level: Middle School

It is the sixth week of class, and Mrs. Reynolds is the newest addition to the eighth-grade algebra department at Lakeview Middle School. She takes a moment from grading papers to look up at her second-period algebra class, which is busy working on this week's test. She pauses in her perusal when she notices Anne looking hopelessly out the window. Mrs. Reynolds waits to make eye contact with Anne, and at that point the student immediately returns to her test. Mrs. Reynolds inwardly sighs in frustration, as this is not the first instance of Anne's lack of attention to her schoolwork.

The next day, Mrs. Reynolds asks the class to quickly make their way to their seats, as they have much to cover before the end of the period. "OK, class, I am going to pass out the test from yesterday . . . ," Mrs. Reynolds begins but is shortly interrupted by William, one of her more boisterous students in the class. "Oh yeah, let me see my grade; I know no one is going to touch my grade this time. I studied my . . . ," but before he can finish his sentence Mrs. Reynolds cuts him off short as she makes a pointed glance at William to stifle further interruptions.

"I am really disappointed in some of you. There are two of you, as I've noted on your tests, whom I need to see after class because your answers look an awful lot alike." Many students begin to giggle and point fingers in the direction of the likely culprits. "However," Mrs. Reynolds continues,

"I don't want to waste class time pointing fingers and complaining about the sorry state of your test scores. We need to keep on schedule and turn to the current lesson today. I don't need to emphasize how important this skill is for the final at the end of the year as well as the upcoming diagnostic tests."

At this point, Mrs. Reynolds has made her way to Anne's desk. Just as she hands Anne her paper, Anne quickly flips it over before anyone can see her grade. Mrs. Reynolds notes that Anne quickly glances around to see if anyone might have noticed her grade.

As Mrs. Reynolds attempts to begin the day's discussion on quadratic equations, she has to make repeated requests for students to put away their test from the day before. She tries to hide her frustration with two students in the back of the classroom who are busy comparing their grades. Once the two students see the teacher's attention is on them, however, they quickly give each other one last friendly shove and then straighten in their seats.

"Now, class, I am going to give you the opportunity to get into your peer groups to work on today's problems. Each group is going to be responsible for one problem from the worksheet." Mrs. Reynolds begins to pass out the worksheet while students move about into their preassigned groups. "I'll give you a moment to look over these problems," Mrs. Reynolds continues, "and then I'll start recording which problems each group volunteers to work on."

Mrs. Reynolds allows the groups to take a few minutes to discuss the worksheets. She circles around to observe Anne's group. The unofficial group leader, Lilly Mitchells, engages the group in her usual take-charge attitude. "I think we should do the fourth problem; it is just like the one we learned about last week and I know we can do it." A couple of the other group members agree, but Mrs. Reynolds notices that Anne remains uninvolved other than to drop her eyes and nod her head in mute acknowledgment.

One of the other group members dares to disagree. "Well, what are we going to learn if we do that? What if one of these other problems is on the next test? I don't know about any of you, but I got a lousy C on yesterday's test." At this point, Mrs. Reynolds notices most of the groups are starting to socialize, and she realizes they have had enough time to consider their choice of problem. She directs the class to begin solving their problems as she makes her way to her desk to finish sorting through some cumulative files.

As the period is about to end, Mrs. Reynolds asks students to make their way back to their original seats. Within moments, the bell rings, and most of the students are off like a shot to make the most of their few precious moments between classes. She notices Anne hesitating in packing up her books and makes her way over to the student. "Anne, is there something amiss? Don't you have to get to your third-period class?"

Anne appears to wrestle with something but then breaks down and begins to unload her worries over her academic performance and her grades in Mrs.

Reynolds's class. "I just can't get another bad grade or my parents will lock me up and throw away the key. I just can't imagine getting in any more trouble than I already am!" Mrs. Reynolds responds, "But, Anne, you have never once asked for my help, and I always notice you staring out the window."

At this point, Anne seems to become quite calm, looks out the window as if concluding something she has been avoiding, and then looks up to respond to Mrs. Reynolds. "I try and try, but it just doesn't matter. I am not good at this algebra stuff, and there is no getting around that. Some people just aren't good at math. I should really ask myself why I even bother."

"Now, hold on a minute, Anne," Mrs. Reynolds interjects. "I know you can do this work. I have faith in you. Plus, look at Loralee, Edith, and Isabelle . . . they are good friends of yours, right? They get strong grades in this class. If they can do it, so can you."

Anne smiles but glances down at her watch, realizing what time it is. "Listen, I appreciate your help, but I don't want to add after-school detention for being tardy to Mr. Lopez's Spanish class to my glorified record."

A month later, Mrs. Reynolds is grading the most recent unit tests. As she gets to Anne's test she skims over the answers and closes her eyes in frustration. Without finishing the grading of the test, she realizes that Anne is going to be less than pleased with the score. She had hoped to see an improvement in Anne's score after their little chat a month prior. But apparently it hadn't made much of a difference. As she looks back on it, she begins to wonder at her naiveté in thinking such superficial feedback would have seriously helped Anne.

Anne clearly had strong perceived inadequacies where this subject matter was concerned, and Anne's sense of hopelessness over the weeks since their chat had only become more evident. Anne hardly ever volunteered to answer questions in class, and she asked for no further help and continued to daydream in class. Even on the few occasions she went to Anne's desk to check up on her work, Anne would make half-hearted attempts without really trying to apply herself to the task. Mrs. Reynolds begins to ask herself what she is supposed to do now. How can she reach this student and help her to see that this situation doesn't have to be as hopeless as it appears?

DISCUSSION QUESTIONS

1. Self-Efficacy
   a. What evidence do you see that Anne suffers from low self-efficacy?
   b. What influences students' efficacy? Do you see evidence of enactive, persuasory, vicarious, or emotive influences as proposed by Bandura's theory on this student's efficacy?

   c. How do beliefs about ability affect a student's motivation? Analyze the role of anxiety in learning. Is anxiety always detrimental to learning?

   d. What attempts has the teacher made for improving Anne's self-efficacy? What additional suggestions would you make for boosting Anne's self-efficacy? How can teachers encourage all students' confidence in their mathematical learning?

   e. What are specific metacognitive or self-regulatory strategies that teachers can share with students that would help students to study more effectively?

   f. What gender differences exist in math self-efficacy? Math anxiety? How does this impact enrollment in math-related college majors?

   g. What is teacher efficacy, and what influence does it have on students' learning? Do you think Mrs. Reynolds has high teacher efficacy?

   h. How is self-efficacy distinct from one's self-esteem?

2. Attributional Theory

   a. What does attributional style refer to, and how does locus of causality apply to motivation?

   b. Classify Anne's attribution along the three dimensions proposed by Weiner.

   c. What is learned helplessness? Do you think Anne's behavior fits into the characteristics of those with learned helplessness?

   d. Outline proven steps Mrs. Reynolds might try to retrain Anne's attributional style.

   e. Compile a list of strategies for how teachers can support self-determination and autonomy in students.

3. Goal Orientations

   a. Regarding the class as a whole, do you see much evidence of students being mastery oriented or performance oriented? What are typical student outcomes associated with each type of goal orientation?

   b. Evaluate whether performance goals are always bad. What is the difference between a performance-approach goal and a performance-avoidance goal?

   c. Evaluate whether mastery goals are always beneficial. What is the difference between a mastery-approach goal and a mastery-avoidance goal? What suggestions would you offer to increase a mastery-orientation approach in this classroom?

   d. Distinguish between incremental and entity views on intelligence. Which does Anne espouse? How do students' views on intelligence influence their mindset for learning?

e. Relate the concept of the meaningfulness of learning to a mastery orientation among students.

f. How can teachers structure the classroom to create more adaptive achievement goals in their students? How do the nature of learning tasks, evaluation and assessment measures, and classroom climate impact students' goals? What does TARGET stand for in looking at students' motivation to learn in school?

4. Assessment

a. Why do students cheat on tests? What strategies might a teacher employ to prevent student cheating?

b. Explain how this teacher's approach to assessment contributed to students being predominantly performance oriented.

c. What assessment strategies would you offer for maximizing student mastery orientation toward learning?

d. What types of authentic assessment might this teacher consider using? What are advantages and disadvantages of more alternative measures of assessment?

e. What advantages might including some measure of self-assessment have for learners? How could teachers successfully incorporate self-assessment into their overall assessment plans?

f. What is the difference between summative and formative assessment? Discuss how both traditional and alternative types of assessment might be utilized for these different goals of assessment.

g. Discuss strategies for communicating with Anne's parents when discussing Anne's performance. Explain how parents and teachers might work together for the benefit of the student.

h. What is the purpose behind diagnostic testing in the school? Evaluate both the benefits of and criticisms to the recent focus on statewide testing. What are the central issues surrounding the accountability and high-stakes testing debate?

Case 11

Stressed Out

Dealing with Academic Pressure in High School

Suggested Theories: Self-Regulation, Social Development, and Personality and
Identity Development
Teacher Challenges: Helping Students with Strategy Use, Lacking Instructional
Time, Student Stress, and Parental Communications and Handling Complaints
Student Level: High School

Evan Rhodes is reviewing the curriculum he will be teaching his eleventh-
grade advanced math students during today's planning period. Grades for
the first quarter just went out, and as he decides which activities and projects
to select for the next quarter he has some concerns about the quality of his
students' performance. Mr. Rhodes has noticed that overall, his students are
struggling to stay focused in class; many aren't taking notes or understanding
underlying key concepts in their workbooks.

Since Mr. Rhodes also teaches advanced tenth-grade math classes, he had
many of these students last year and knows that they excel at setting goals for
their performance, supervising their understanding of the lessons, and using
various study tactics—often reevaluating when techniques proved ineffective.
However, as the second quarter in the academic year gets under way, he also
doesn't believe they are using higher order learning strategies to study as
reflected in their word-problem answers; instead, he feels they are regressing
to using more basic repetition-type study tactics.

Mr. Rhodes has witnessed his students slipping into a more passive role
when they correct their homework answers from the answers he puts on the
board; he sees they do so now with little to no discussion or verbalizations
of their computations. Additionally, he has observed behavioral changes as
well that are changing the atmosphere of the class. In general, students are
having increasing difficulty getting along with each other. Some students are

87

acting very irritable, others are showing little patience, some are demonstrating a lack of self-control, and others are lethargic. This is all leading to class disruptions.

He wonders what the cause could be for the downward spiral in these students, and he is determined to assist them. Mr. Rhodes is deep in thought when his colleague, Julieta Cabrera, comes into his class. "Hi, Julieta," he says, a little surprised he didn't hear her come in. "Hey, Evan! I see you've got your concentration face on, so you must be worried about something important," Julieta says lightheartedly. Evan laughs in response and discusses with Julieta the troubles with his eleventh graders. Julieta has been an incredible asset to him this year since she has years of experience with eleventh graders and he is new to this grade.

After listening to Evan intently, Julieta replies sympathetically, "Unfortunately, what you are seeing in the classroom reflects what is happening in their personal lives and is common to juniors at this time of the year. Many students are in the process of getting college applications completed while taking standardized tests and touring universities. So while continuing to keep up with their current schoolwork, they must also make room to think about and prepare for their future. I changed a few of my deadlines because I realized how many of my students were going to be touring schools in those weeks and I felt it was unfair to have them also do a major project—waiting a few weeks made all the difference in their competency on that assignment. And don't forget, these kids also have extracurricular activities like sports, music, school clubs, after-school jobs, responsibilities at home . . . the list is endless, and I believe they start to realize that what worked in the ninth and tenth grades has to be adjusted if they are to have enough time to fit it all in! It's what adjustments they make that is the key."

Evan thanks Julieta for this insight and believes she is exactly right; his students are making alterations in their learning tactics, but he feels those new methods could prove costly and considers it his duty to aid them.

As Evan walks to his car that afternoon after school, his thoughts are interrupted by the sound of someone calling his name. "Mr. Rhodes," one of his advanced math students calls out tentatively. "Yes, hi, Corrine. What can I do for you?" Mr. Rhodes replies amicably as he walks over to where the student is sitting. "Well, I wanted to talk to you before I talked to the guidance counselor about maybe moving to a lower math class. I no longer think I'm as good at math as everyone always told me I was . . . it's obvious I can't cut it in your class," Corrine answers distressed.

"Really? You think you are not doing well? May I ask why you think this?" Mr. Rhodes asks surprised. Corrine tells him she has been struggling in the class to make straight As and that her recent SAT math score was lower than either she or her parents expected. She says her parents were outraged, believing she must not have taken preparing for the SAT seriously and, consequently, enrolled her in private math classes on the weekend. She says she doubts she would be able to pass the advanced placement test that students in this course take to earn college credit—proving she's just not that good.

Mr. Rhodes is astonished to hear of Corrine's newfound belief that she is not good in math because she is one of the most industrious students in the class, and while she hasn't earned perfect scores on all assignments, her average in the course is still an A.

Monday morning arrives, and Mr. Rhodes comes prepared to implement some of the ideas he spent his weekend devising. "Alright, class, let's start today with a brief exchange of ideas, and please keep an open mind," Mr. Rhodes says while looking over his students. He points to the large image of a gas tank that is being projected on the whiteboard from his computer screen. The gas tank has a needle that looks just like that on a car's gas tank; however, in this example there are three areas: *Empty, Just Right, Overdrive*. His students look from him to the gas tank image, seeming a bit perplexed and somewhat amused.

"Before you raise your hands to poke fun at me for treating you like little kids, think about this gas tank as an analogy that describes your body's energy reserves." Even though many students chuckle, he sees he has their undivided attention. "OK, so I noticed some of you are not acting in the same manner that you did when the school year began, and I think it's important for your success in this class, as well as for the class's climate, that we look to resolve it. So let me see a show of hands of how many feel that your engines, your bodies, are functioning in the *Just Right* area, where you know you feel easily able to concentrate on your assignments."

Mr. Rhodes sees that no hands have been raised, confirming his suspicions regarding stress and his students' performance. One student shouts, "I was there last year!" causing laughter throughout the class. Mr. Rhodes laughs quietly and continues, "Alright, how many of you think that your bodies are functioning in the *Empty* area, where you feel tired and in need of a constant energy boost?" While hesitantly at first, students' hands begin to rise. "Good. Now, I think we're on to something. Anyone care to share why they think they're on *Empty*?"

Mr. Rhodes calls on Luna. "Well, I think it's because I've been trying to keep my grades up while at the same time focusing on all the college possibilities. Not only that, but me and my parents are stressed out coming up with plans for how I'll pay for college if I don't get the scholarship amounts I need, and since I'm trying to get scholarships, I'm strained about my grades staying high . . . and, well, I'm beyond tired." More students describe scenarios like Luna's, and one student hits upon an interesting point about feeling guilt. Mr. Rhodes decides to probe further.

Given they are high-achieving students, they enjoy learning and are accustomed to knowledge giving them internal satisfaction. However, their present time demands have forced them to cut corners when studying, which means reduced goal setting, more repetition, little to no connections to prior learning, and less chance at retention. The result is that while their scores on tests may remain high, they don't feel they are gaining as much out of the work because as many put it, they are just doing enough to get by and they fear it will affect them later down the road when they don't remember the information or can't connect it to what they are learning.

Mr. Rhodes presses his students further. "And where has feeling guilty or frustrated with your new study methods put you—the *Empty, Just Right,* or *Overdrive* area? How is that perhaps indicative of some of the behavior problems we are seeing now in this class?"

Deion raises his hand, and when Mr. Rhodes nods for him to speak, he says, "Well, I would say for me it's the overdrive area because I do feel like there's so much going on that I can't focus, like I can't get everything to slow down a little. I feel guilty about not having been better at finding time to study the way I used to and get the highest A, which is what I am used to, which makes me, I don't know, annoyed? So then I come down hard on myself for not doing my best, and I punish myself, you know, like I won't go hang out and shoot hoops. I'm on edge all the time, and like last week when Asher here started messing around with me I got angry fast."

Deion playfully shoves Asher, who is seated next to him, on the shoulder as the students laugh. Asher then adds, "I'm glad you are on overdrive man, but between schoolwork, SAT test prep class, my after-school job, lacrosse practices, and figuring out where I want to go to school, and my parents constantly on my case to make sure I don't miss a deadline or suggesting another school I hadn't thought of, I'm on the empty side like Luna. I'm so tired all the time that I know that if I close my eyes for even a minute I am going to start snoring in class."

Many students nod and agree throughout the room. More discussion ensues about how strictly the majority of these students feel they must stick to their planned path to success, and many share stories of how they feel they have been preparing for college since they were little. Others say that they are fulfilling a dream of either being the first in their family to go to college, or finally being able to follow in a parent's footsteps, or how they want to ensure they do not let their parents down since many discussed how much their parents have invested in ensuring they have a bright future.

While many of them cite feeling stressed about missing out on social events or hanging out with friends whose career path is not as strict as theirs, they still feel that they are doing the right thing and for the right reasons. Mr. Rhodes thanks his students for their insight and promises to get back to them as to changes in the class; then he begins that day's lesson.

After school that day Evan is reflecting on his advanced math class's responses, feeling satisfied that they'd been able to freely reveal their frustrations. Together through the exercise they were able to identify some of the factors affecting their classroom performance and behavior that will help him in implementing his new plans for the class. Evan is sure that switching instructional gears and explicitly engaging his students in meaningful learning and enhanced strategy instruction will help them become more adept at using intricate study methods.

He thinks the students can soon resume learning meaningfully and in turn, alleviating their sense of guilt and some of their frustration—a winning situation for his classroom climate. Evan knows that this will mean reducing instructional time spent on the concepts; however, he believes the benefits outweigh the costs and that they can make up the difference in instructional time with an insignificant increase in homework.

In addition, Evan has decided to move up a large and engaging problem-based learning community service project that he originally scheduled for the end of the year, to coordinate with the strategy instruction. Since the project requires students to set goals, self-monitor, time manage, and self-evaluate to be successful with the project, Evan feels it is a perfect way to use the project's goals as a way to reinforce what he's working on with them in daily lessons.

A few weeks later, Evan is in a meeting with the school's principal, Mrs. Franklin. "Evan, thank you for meeting with me under such short notice; I appreciate it," Mrs. Franklin says considerately. "I called this meeting to discuss some recent concerns that have been brought to my attention regarding your eleventh-grade advanced math students," Mrs. Franklin says as she reaches for her glasses and opens a file folder. "Now, you know I prefer that teachers and parents communicate with each other and come to an understanding; however, in this case, I felt it best to meet with you because I've had more than half of the parents in that class contact me with concerns."

"In fact," she continues, "these are concerns they say have been communicated to you but still have not been addressed. The more troubling allegations are ones that are centered around the curriculum for the class. First, the parents claim you're not teaching the course content according to the standards for the class in favor of devoting a large amount of class time to teaching strategies, strategies that they believe their children possess but would rather not use because they are time consuming. Thus, they maintain you have assigned all the work not completed in class for homework, which has added a significant amount of time to each day.

"Second, the parents feel that you assigned a lengthy project requiring time in the classroom and after class but gave no notice. Parents contend that the project counts for a hefty portion of the students' grades but that the project's connection to the curriculum is neither apparent nor explained. You can understand some parents' concerns—all they hear about is how important it is for their kids to master identified standards and ace statewide testing."

Evan sits back in his chair, exhaling a breath of frustration. He feels deflated upon hearing that all of his efforts to help his students are misconstrued as incompetence on his part.

DISCUSSION QUESTIONS

1. Self-Regulated Learning
   a. What is self-regulated learning and how is it important for educational success? What are the main components or elements of popular models of self-regulation? Do you feel students are experiencing difficulties in the forethought, performance, or self-reflection phase of self-regulation? Or in another model, the self-observation, self-judgment, or self-reaction phase?
   b. Examine Mr. Rhodes's engine analogy regarding self-regulation. Was it an effective method for attaining his intended goal? How else can teachers get at identifying causes or problems in students having problems with self-regulation?
   c. Judge Mr. Rhodes's attempt to instruct his students on the use of strategies as a way to increase self-regulation.
   d. Critique Mr. Rhodes's choice to coordinate the large project with the instruction of strategies. Do you believe it would be beneficial in improving the students' self-regulation for the class?
   e. Discuss how students in the case are demonstrating self-regulation about future college plans. Speculate as to why the students in Mr. Rhodes's class chose to self-regulate some behaviors over others? How does motivation play a role in their decision?
   f. Discuss examples of self-monitoring and self-reinforcement components to self-regulation shown in the case. How did this impact students' behavior?
   g. Students with disabilities often struggle with comprehension monitoring and rely on others. Discuss the importance of teachers' being able to identify students who have learning disabilities, and speculate on how teachers can assist students with learning disabilities so they may self-regulate successfully.
   h. How is Corrine demonstrating poor self-monitoring regarding her math ability? How is it affecting her self-efficacy in math? How has her belief that she can no longer meet the goal of passing the college-credit exam contributed to her low self-efficacy? How can teachers help a student like Corrine?
   i. How might a teacher encourage students' self-regulated learning skills? How might a teacher encourage students' self-assessment of their learning?

j. What role do you see parents in this case playing in their adolescents' self-regulation?

2. Social Development
   a. How can stress and external pressures for future success affect an adolescent's self-concept and self-esteem? Discuss examples in this case where this is observed.
   b. Do you see evidence of how others' opinions of an adolescent as well as their expectations can affect an adolescent's self-concept and self-esteem in the case?
   c. Speculate on how teenagers' plans may not come to fruition due to outside forces and how the dissolution of these plans may affect their social and emotional well-being.
   d. Discuss how students' rejection of social events, in lieu of their inflexible future plans, affects their social development and peer status.
   e. The teacher in this case notices how the students' changing environments have affected their social relationships in the class. Discuss the various examples introduced in the case and how continued conflict can impact the students' social relationships.
   f. Discuss how you could apply Bronfenbrenner's ecological systems theory to the students in this case. Which of Bronfenbrenner's ecological systems may best explain social development in this case?

3. Identity Development
   a. Which of Erikson's stages of psychosocial development are these students likely to be in? How is the students' focus on future plans impacting the stage's resolution?
   b. What about students who choose not to pursue college after high school? What personal, environmental, or societal influences impact an adolescent's choice to pursue either college or a vocational track after high school? What pressures might these students be under?
   c. Deliberate on how the teacher in this case is aiding his students in a positive resolution of the challenge that they experience in this stage.
   d. Discuss how perfectionism can impact an adolescent's personality.
   e. Speculate on the negative effects that parental and social pressures can have on an adolescent's identity. How can it lead to establishment of a negative identity? How can it lead to rebellion and unhappiness?
   f. Discuss the stages of Marcia's identity status that you see in this case.

4. Parental Complaints
   a. In this case, the principal alludes to parental complaints that went unresolved. How can teachers most effectively handle parental complaints? Discuss ideas/suggestions for teachers to handle challenges from parents about their choices for instructional approaches.

b. Do you think it is fair for parents to question Mr. Rhodes's decisions regarding strategy instruction? Why or why not?

c. Outline ways in which the situation with parental concerns that occurred in this case might have been avoided. What can be done now? Overall, why is it beneficial to have an open line of communication between parents and teachers?

d. This case presents parents who appear to be overinvolved. How can overinvolved parents create discomfort in the learning environment?

e. How can professional development be geared to helping teachers to effectively handle challenging parents?

Part V

CLASSROOM MANAGEMENT

Case 12

The Role of the Teacher

Can Students and Teachers Be Friends?

Suggested Theories: Classroom Management, Social Cognitive Theory, and
Cognitive and Moral Development
Teacher Challenges: Social Media, Engaging Older High School Students,
Using Technology Appropriately in the Classroom, Plagiarism and Cheating,
and Teacher-Student Interactions
Student Level: High School

Mr. Bauer has finished taking attendance and begins the day's lecture in
his twelfth-grade psychology class. This is the period after lunch, and he sees
that there are several students who have yet to arrive but whom he has seen
around the school earlier in the day—this is not an uncommon occurrence in
his class. He figures that as long as they attend and do not disrupt the class
when they come in, he doesn't worry too much about tardiness and never
penalizes his students like other teachers do.

After the lesson concludes, Mr. Bauer conducts an exam review of some
of the concepts the students will be studying for their upcoming exam. This
exam review is a favorite activity among his students because they feel it is
engaging and best of all, very fun. Mr. Bauer places short real-life scenarios
in a bucket, and one by one students pick a scenario that they will then try
to match to one of the vocabulary concepts they are studying. This way they
learn the concepts using real-world examples.

Since the end of the school year is near, Mr. Bauer feels it is especially
important to employ interesting and innovative assignments and activities. In
all of his years of teaching, he knows that one thing is for certain—keeping
students engaged who are about to graduate is challenging—even in a popular
elective class like his. Senioritis is a very real affliction among seniors, and
it is widespread especially with all of the end of the year events approaching.

Many students have one foot out the door and begin to lose sight of the importance of completing work and coming to class because they feel they are moving on to bigger and better things.

After the class ends, the students in Mr. Bauer's class are exiting his class headed for their lockers. Best friends Harper, Emma, and Kingsley are chatting amicably. Harper says, "Isn't Mr. Bauer a riot? I swear, I wish all the teachers in this school were like him! I follow him on Instagram and his posts are hilarious!" Emma and Kingsley exchange worried glances. Emma then says, "I agree he is really funny, and he definitely cares that we are entertained in his class while we learn . . . but I don't know, I think he sometimes focuses on fun and we all get so sidetracked that we don't learn a whole lot and then end up having to do so much at home."

Kingsley adds, "Yeah, I think so too, like today with the exam review. We got sidetracked when Mateo chose the one about the celebrity crush because Mr. Bauer let him go on and on, and he let all the other guys talk about theirs too!" The girls all nod and Harper says, "Yeah, I see your point. Guess we all got into it because he's just hot and—let's be honest, ladies—we all wanted to know who he's crushing on!" They all chuckle, and Emma says, "True, but then do you all even remember what the psychology term was we were supposed to review that went with that scenario? One of the big five personality traits? Or wait, was it Erikson's theory?"

Kingsley answers, "No clue! So it's like we didn't really review. It's like that with everything in his class though. I mean we've all been accepted to college, but still we have to keep our grades up so that means doing well." Harper agrees with her friends but says, "OK . . . OK . . . you all are getting me worried. We are a couple of months away from high school freedom, so can we please focus on something important, like this morning's Instagram posts? I mean, did you see who started dating over the weekend?" The girls giggle and look with interest at Harper's phone before going to their next class.

The next day, the students in Mr. Bauer's class are working on the computers researching their upcoming famous psychologist presentations. "Hey, Mr. Bauer, can I wear a fake beard and mustache to the presentation so I can look like my psychologist, Sigmund Freud?" asks one student pointing to the picture on the screen. Others start joking around by saying they too want to bring in props. Mr. Bauer thinks it's a great idea and joins in their discussion suggesting various ideas for each psychologist.

Kingsley and Emma are seated next to each other on the computers exploring different websites on their psychologists while quietly chatting. Harper brings a chair over to sit with her friends. "Did you all see where they are instead of being at school?" Harper says pointing to her phone, which is displaying a picture on a social media site of a group of kids at the beach.

"Seriously, I'm a little jealous. They're working on their tan while I'm getting to know more about Carl Jung. Ooh, but I love Tara's new bathing suit!" Emma says indicating one of their friends who is on the screen.

Harper replies, "I know, it's kinda revealing though for Tara! I bet she got it though because she wants to get Dedrick to notice her. She says she always sees him commenting online when girls wear those types of suits. Let's show her some support in case she gets hateful comments." Kingsley agrees but grabs Harper's arm and says unbelievingly, "Don't comment on their photo right now! We're in school! Put the phone away before we all get in trouble!"

Harper looks over her shoulder and points in the direction of Mr. Bauer. "Relax! It's Mr. Bauer! Besides he can't see the phone because my back is to him, and anyhow he doesn't care what we do as long as we look like we're getting work done. Have you ever heard him yell at anyone? I mean look over there," Harper says pointing to a group of students whose computer screens are showing webpages that are not on the subject of the class before continuing. "Do they look like they are researching psychologists?"

The girls all look over to where Harper is pointing and see not just the group she's pointing out but other classmates that are on YouTube watching funny videos and on social media. Mr. Bauer is chatting with a few students over by his desk completely unaware, it seems, of what is going on in the rest of the class. Emma sighs and says, "Yeah, I have to agree with Harper; he is one of the most laid-back teachers ever. You know, I don't think many kids turn work in on time. I was over at Chase's house the other day, and I saw he was still working on that comparative theory assignment . . . you know the one that was due like last month, right? When I asked him about it," she continues, "he said he got Mr. Bauer to give him extra time because it's volleyball season and he's so busy with practices and games."

Kingsley shakes her head and says, "Really? I guess that makes sense because I had heard from students in his other periods that when they got sick he gave them forever to make up the work with no late penalties . . . but it sounds like he does that regardless; you just have to ask him."

Harper adds in, "Yep, I know that to be true because when my family and I went to California for my cousin's wedding, I missed a week of school. Mr. Bauer told me to make up the work as soon as I was able to but never gave me strict deadlines, and he was really easy grading. There was an assignment that I forgot to finish, but I lied a little and told him I had given him the wrong version; he just told me to get him the right version by the end of the week! Fabulous guy! Now, enough talk about Mr. Bauer . . . Emma do fill us in on your and Chase's plan for how you'll continue being lovebirds while going to different universities."

The girls laugh and seeing that Mr. Bauer had not said anything to anyone for being off task, Emma and Kingsley decide to take a break from their research to talk more with Harper.

Later that week, Mr. Bauer is inputting his grades into the school's online grade book during his planning period. He knows his students are going to be pleased with their recent exam scores, as most of the class did well. He did notice when he was grading his students' exams that many of them had answered very similarly for some of the essay questions. The thought of cheating quickly crosses his mind because he knows that he is not one to ever watch his students too carefully during an exam. He knows they are all good kids, and he doesn't think that they would risk cheating this close to the end of the school year.

He also remembers something like this occurring earlier in the year and the students telling him that many of them study together—it would certainly make sense that if they study together that they would have similar answers. In addition, Mr. Bauer doesn't change his exams much from year to year, and since there are many students who have older siblings who have taken his class, it is also possible that the older brothers and sisters are helping them study—even if away at college.

Since he is considered to be friendly with most of his students, they share with him how they video chat with their older siblings about school, friends, and relationships. Sometimes, he even has to admit, they may overshare but as long as nothing is inappropriate, Mr. Bauer feels that it is important to be able to listen to his students and know what interests and motivates them. This way he can relate much better to them and infuse current events and trends into his lessons to make them relatable to them.

That afternoon when Emma, Harper, and Kingsley are driving home from school they're discussing the two assignments Mr. Bauer just returned. "I am so thrilled with my grade—100 percent on both the test and the paper! Woohoo! And, Kingsley, you were only a couple of points behind me! And, Harper, what did you get, like a high B on both?" Emma exclaims proudly. "Definitely! This week was super tough with all the tests and papers. This calls for a celebration!" Harper replies elatedly.

The girls agree and begin making plans for the weekend. "Hey, Tara's texting asking for us to meet her and Aisha at Ally's Frozen Yogurt. We in?" Kingsley asks looking at Emma driving and Harper in the backseat. "Sure!" the two girls say in unison, and Kingsley texts their friends back letting them know they'll meet them shortly.

At the frozen yogurt store, the girls sit with their friends Tara and Aisha on the store's outside patio area. The girls' conversation naturally moves to this week's schoolwork. Kingsley asks Tara and Aisha how they did on Mr. Bauer's test and paper they got back this week. Aisha says she is thrilled with her As, and Tara answers, "An A and B+, so I cannot complain!" Then Tara lowers her voice before continuing, "Did you all hear though about the students in our class who turned in papers that weren't theirs or that they basically copied off the Internet?" Harper nods, acknowledging she knew, and Aisha, Kingsley, and Emma seem surprised.

Shocked, Aisha says, "I had no idea! Really? But then again you know with me being new here maybe I'm just out of the loop." The girls giggle and Emma answers incredulously, "Well, I think it's safe to say that we've all heard rumors about students doing that in some classes, but I guess I just thought there wasn't really much truth to the rumors. I mean Mr. Bauer is lenient, but are you saying he knows they're cheating and doesn't punish them? Or does he just not catch them? Because today, in our class, he said the average on both the papers and the exam had been good."

Tara is first to respond and says, "Yeah, he said the same thing in our period. But I happen to know it's true about students turning in others' work, and I heard this has been going on for a long time. Other teachers have suggested he run plagiarism software on his papers, but I guess he doesn't seem to think there's a problem." Harper interjects sarcastically, "I'm willing to bet these students get high scores too. I think it happens with many of his tests too because I heard if you know someone who had him before you can study off their tests and you're golden! Makes sense why some breeze through the tests if they came in already knowing what the questions were."

The girls agree that he's too nice and that he probably thinks he is a good teacher and that is why students do well, not that they are cheating. Aisha asks sheepishly, "If this has been going on for a while, why doesn't someone say something to the principal?" Kingsley replies, "Well, I think that no one wants to be known as the whistle-blower, especially because, thanks to social media, the news of who came forward would spread like wildfire and it would be social suicide—especially since many of the kids suspected are popular."

They all agree and then also discuss how a possible cheating scandal could affect college acceptances, so they think that it would be a lot to bear for someone to want to risk by speaking to the administration. Aisha says, "I may sound like a total geek and it certainly makes life easier now to cut corners, but I am not risking my future for a dumb assignment. I'd rather just do it. Besides, when we get to college, you can't count on having professors like Mr. Bauer."

Emma answers, "It's true. My older brother warned me about the plagiarism in college. He told us a story last year, remember, Kingsley? That kid in his dorm who cheated?" Emma pauses while Kingsley nods, "Yeah, not good, and professors are not so lenient with deadlines and missed assignments. It's better we learn now to get things done on time than have it hit us all in a few months and then flunk out of college because we can't handle the pressure.

I'm with Aisha; I'd rather do my own work and learn. Even if it does mean I have to cut this fun time short because I have to get home and start my physics homework so I can hang out this weekend."

All the students regrettably agree that they have to get going, and they start throwing away their trash. Aisha, who is having people over on Saturday for her birthday, shouts out a reminder of the time they're all to come over. Harper asks, "So, Aisha, who all did you end up inviting? I know you were nervous to invite some people in a clique but leave others out—fearing the social media fallout." Aisha looks nervous but replies with false bravado, "Well . . . all of you of course!" the girls laugh as she rattles off more names.

Harper says, "Well, that is going to be a blast! I do thank you as the one single girl among you all for inviting the fine guys you just named!" All the girls laugh since Harper is known for being a serial dater. Aisha says hesitantly, "I did try to do my best with the different cliques and totally went over the number of people I wanted to invite . . . Tara helped me with the list but . . . to be honest, I am a little scared of the drama. I mean I haven't even gone to some of these parties, but the pictures on Instagram I've seen look amazing! Hope I can make mine just as great . . . you know, without the hateful comments some people get on social media."

Emma replies sympathetically, "Well, if it helps you feel any better I already saw some pictures from students at local shops trying on various outfits for your party! Try not to focus too much on the negative comments because that can happen after every party, every date, every trip to the mall . . . it's just out there. Remember earlier this week when we all went for coffee and got those new lattes before school and Harper posted a picture of us with our lattes?"

Kingsley says she remembers, but Harper adds annoyed, "Yeah, I do because Emma and Kingsley got off scot-free, but me, I got hurtful comments about my weight! Oh, and the shirt I was wearing because it said #fabulous. Really, because what I wear was directly related to what was seemingly my poor choice in beverage?" Kingsley says dismissingly, "Do not even listen to that stuff you all! It's just the nature of social media . . . you gotta take the good with the bad!" Harper replies still miffed, "And what exactly was the good there? Cute emoji and comments like 'beautiful girls' that were addressed to you two?"

Emma quickly replies while putting her arm around Harper, "Nope, that we found out from my friend in ballet that the vanilla flavor was the best one and it gave us an excuse to stop by there again the next morning . . . and see the cute barista . . . who, I may add, flirted with you!" Harper seems to have shed her bad mood instantly at the happy memory, and all the girls laugh, Tara and Aisha wanting to know more about the barista as they walk through the parking lot in search of their cars.

The next day in Mr. Bauer's class, the students are involved in a question-and-answer session for their upcoming famous psychologist presentations.

Mr. Bauer wants to make sure that everyone is on the right track. Mr. Bauer has already met with several students who needed help and helped them completely reframe their papers as well as gave them many great websites from which to pull their research. He felt great when his students showered him with thanks and told him how wonderful it was to have a teacher assist them so much. They went on to say that is why he is one of the favorite teachers in the school!

Mr. Bauer thinks how it always makes his day to hear how much his students like him! Mr. Bauer notices that shortly into the review session that many students are distracted and looking at their phones. He then quickly looks over to the wall where the bathroom passes are hanging and sees they are all missing. He wonders if once again he is having female students in the bathroom gossiping about one another and posting on social media. He was alerted to this situation by another teacher who saw the Twitter feeds on her students' accounts as she was asking them to put their phones away, and she noted the time coincided with his class time.

Mr. Bauer knows that a student in one of his classes, Aisha, had a party this weekend and this was all the students were discussing, especially because a popular couple broke up after one of the students got back together with an ex that was at the party. He wonders if this is what could be happening—yet not sure what he could do about it. He can't monitor his students in the bathroom, and as long as they don't take too much time he really doesn't feel it is his place to say anything—he feels that social media, like anything else going on these days, is something students need to learn to maneuver and deal with the repercussions on their own.

Mr. Bauer's thoughts are brought back to the question-and-answer session by Mateo, a student who is asking if there is any way that he can postpone the presentations a week. "It's just that some of us have the math team tournament to compete in, and if we make it we go to state championships next week and that will look awesome for college! It's just a lot you know!" Mateo says visibly frustrated. Soon, other students began shouting out reasons for moving the presentations.

Mr. Bauer knows his students are dealing with the stress of having to have one foot in their future world and one foot still here—it is one of the reasons he has always been lenient with his due dates for assignments and his checking of their grammar and spelling. He doesn't want to add extra stress; as long as they do the work, learn the concepts, and take advantage of the word processing program's capabilities to correct their work, he feels that is acceptable—after all he is not an English teacher.

As always, Mr. Bauer wants the students to do well, and it does sound like there are many things going on over the next two weeks. So he decides to give them all extra time and move the presentations back to the end of the month. All the students cheer, and he can see they are taking to social media to announce to everyone the change, telling him how awesome he is and how much they love his class. Mr. Bauer beams at the compliment and knows he did the right thing! The important thing is they are learning about psychology and enjoying the process along the way.

DISCUSSION QUESTIONS

1. Classroom Management and Use of Technology in the Classroom
   a. What type of classroom management approach is this teacher using? How has his classroom management been affected by the grades of students he teaches?
   b. How can a teacher choosing to play the role of friend, rather than authority figure to their students, have advantages and disadvantages? What disadvantages are shown here in the case?
   c. Identify misconceptions that some students may form regarding what may be considered acceptable behavior, as well appropriate policies and procedures in the classroom, as a result of being in Mr. Bauer's classroom? What dangers could this pose for these students' academic future at a college or university?
   d. Does Mr. Bauer demonstrate "withitness" in the classroom? How is that evident in the case? If he is not showing "withitness," formulate ways in which he could.
   e. Critique this teacher's methods for handling his student's Internet use in the classroom. Outline some potential concerns that his methods could cause for students' academic well-being.
   f. Discuss some of the dangers that can exist when students learn to cheat the system or to use loopholes to complete work that are acts of plagiarism.
   g. Because these are high school seniors, what discussions would be expected to occur in the classroom regarding Internet plagiarism and intellectual ownership? How can these discussions help to prepare them for their transition into the workforce and/or college? Would school-wide policies on academic honesty be effective here?
   h. Generate strategies or tactics that teachers should be consistently employing when choosing to either incorporate technology into their students' assignments or when allowing their students use of technology in their classrooms.

2. Social Cognitive Theory and Observational Learning
   a. Describe how elements of Bandura's social cognitive theory are taking place in this case.

b. Identify examples of observational learning that could take place when students see that others are being allowed to get away with making their own due dates for work or for cheating.

c. What role does social reinforcement such as likes in social media or negative comments play in shaping students' behaviors? What evidence do you see of the effects of social media in this case?

d. In general, what role can teachers play in being positive role models for their students? While the teacher in the case is well liked by the students, why could he not be considered a positive role model? How can teachers expose students to positive symbolic models?

e. Outline examples from the case in which the students are learning via response facilitation. Do you believe these examples to be positive ones? How can this teacher use inhibition/disinhibition in his class to help students' negative actions?

f. Explain how vicarious reinforcement can occur in situations like the ones in the case where students are observing negative behaviors. How can these negative learned academic behaviors pose threats to students' futures?

g. What is self-regulated learning, and which event in the case do you see this relate to? How can students' academic behaviors be affected by social pressures to fit in with the group as well as to present themselves online in a way that others approve?

3. Effects of Social Media
   a. What overall challenges are teachers faced with in the classroom due to students' interest in social media? What strategies can you devise that could assist the teachers?

   b. How is social media assisting students in engaging and in learning negative behaviors? What dangers does this pose for adolescent bullying, depression, or withdrawal?

   c. Explain how students' behaviors in the case are affected by how they will be viewed on social media. Compare and contrast the different student reactions to social media comments. Generate possible explanations for those reactions.

   d. One of the students in the case is experiencing fear as to how her upcoming party will be viewed when compared to other social events that she hasn't attended but has seen on social media. Outline some of the problems that adolescents can face in trying to live up to the unrealistic expectations manifested on other people's social media.

   e. Discuss the explanations that the students pose for why no one is likely to come forward and report the apparent cheating epidemic that is occurring in this teacher's class. How is social media playing a role in maintaining the silence?

4. Cognitive Development and Moral Development in Adolescence
   a. What role might adolescent egocentrism play in the decision making and behaviors that the students are exhibiting in this case? How could it also relate to students' decisions of engaging in dishonest behavior?
   b. How can social media's ability to spread a rumor instantly or the instant gratification that earning likes on adolescents' social media post impact adolescent egocentrism? What effects would this pose for the classroom?
   c. Discuss strategies or tactics in which teachers can assist students in reducing their adolescent egocentrism. How could the teacher's classroom management approach in this case help to extend adolescent egocentrism?
   d. Discuss the role that social media plays in adolescents' cognitive development. How may it impede, rather than assist, adolescents' cognitive growth?
   e. According to Kohlberg's theory of moral development, determine the level and stage that the students in this case are functioning in. Support your answer with examples from the case.
   f. Imagine that this situation occurred in your classroom; generate examples of developmentally appropriate strategies that you could use for managing plagiarism.

5. Plagiarism and Cheating Prevention: Teachers and Schools
   a. What types of school services or assistance can schools/teachers offer students who are getting ready to graduate to ensure that they stay on track? How can teachers and schools ensure students are educated about the consequences that cheating and plagiarism may have on their acceptance into college?
   b. How can teachers and schools help high school seniors to better handle the stress and the realities of transitioning from high school to college?
   c. Outline ideas about the consequences and expectations that a school should clearly communicate in their student manual about academic honesty. Should plagiarism detection services be employed?
   d. Explain how refraining from recycling the use of assignments from year to year and creating assignments that cannot easily be copied may help to prevent or discourage plagiarism. What innovative assignments might teachers employ that would make it more difficult for students to recycle previously submitted assignments or copy from the Internet?
   e. Generate ideas for what fair and reasonable consequences are for students who are caught cheating, both for an individual teacher and school-wide.

Case 13

Responding to Students'
Back Talk and Disrespect

Suggested Theories: Operant Conditioning, Classroom Management,
Motivation, and Adolescent Development
Teacher Challenges: Motivating Students, Back Talk and Disrespect from Students,
Defiance and Student Refusal to Follow Instructions, and Power Struggles
Student Level: Middle School

Mr. Jackson came into teaching as a second career, so he taught for only a couple of years at a small middle school in the Midwest until his wife's promotion relocated them to a city in the South. Mr. Jackson's new job is teaching eighth-grade literature at a large suburban middle school. Mr. Jackson has had little trouble adjusting, for he has encountered friendly coworkers and a positive working environment. He has been using most of the lessons that he has taught in the past. He was excited to introduce his Shakespeare project because this was always one of the assignments that Mr. Jackson's previous students had thoroughly enjoyed.

The assignment is centered on William Shakespeare's tragedies, comedies, and histories. Each group has a set of plays that they analyze and discuss before preparing classroom presentations. Mr. Jackson encourages creativity in their presentations, suggesting they use their imaginations for props, costumes, and artifacts. Students choose from a range of presentation options such as comparing different scenes, acting out portions of scenes, and analyzing how a theme can influence the entire play. Mr. Jackson also has each group create twenty questions from which he will choose a few to be part of the class's final exam.

He has not heard any complaints; however, he also has not seen much enthusiasm since the project began last week. He wonders whether he should have made that last-minute decision to change when the assignment is offered in the school year because he is now a bit concerned, having looked at the data in his "progress checks" assessing students' advancement. Thus far, he has performed two progress checks, and students are not performing well. Three out of the five groups are further behind than expected, and frankly, Mr. Jackson is beginning to worry that they may not catch up. Mr. Jackson supposes that it was an error on his part to not consider the possibility that the students in his new school would think any differently of the assignment.

An example of Mr. Jackson's dilemma is group five, who was assigned *The Merchant of Venice, A Midsummer Night's Dream*, and *The Taming of the Shrew*. The group has four students, Gloria, Stacey, Joel, and Eli. Although other students have been diligently working on this assignment for the better part of two weeks, this group has barely finished the introductions for each of their plays. Mr. Jackson is aware of the problem, although he is exasperated with them for not getting the work done. Last week, Stacey earned three detentions for not paying attention, for refusing to return to her seat, and for throwing a pocket mirror at Joel.

Unfortunately, this seems to be an ongoing issue with Stacey. He is unsure of the best way to deal with the amount of back talk she gives in her attempt to avoid doing what he asks in the classroom, although he knows from her work that she may also be struggling with the content. Her defiance may stem not only from the adolescent need for independence but also from her feeling that she can't excel in the class work. In contrast, Joel has made it clear to Mr. Jackson that he is not interested in English because he is focused on math and science, so he constantly works on assignments for other teachers and neglects the assignments that Mr. Jackson hands out.

Conversely, Mr. Jackson believes Eli to be a good student but finds he is unmotivated and procrastinates until the last possible chance. Eli also is almost compulsive about online gaming with his friends at school and gets sidetracked discussing gaming situations with other classmates who will listen. Gloria, on the other hand, is driven and often scores very highly on her assignments yet does not seem to be performing at her usual level. Mr. Jackson decides to take the weekend to think of some effective techniques that he can introduce to his classes that will boost morale regarding the assignment and keep his students' interest on their work.

Mr. Jackson greets his students the following Monday and explains that he has added a few things to reward the students who are staying on track. At this point, he notices that Stacey has arrived late to class. He makes eye contact with her, but other than a disrespectful look and demeanor that seems to convey "so what if I'm late, what are you going to do about it?" she doesn't say anything. He notes her tardy before continuing to address the class. He announces that from now on, he will perform daily progress checks. For every satisfactory progress check that a student earns, he or she will receive one bonus point toward his or her project.

In addition, he explains that if a student accumulates ten consecutive checks, then he or she will also receive a homework pass. The homework pass can be used at any time to replace any homework assignment without penalty. The students seemed pleased and most nod their heads and smile at Mr. Jackson's new rules. "Cool, Mr. Jackson. Are we gonna get a little kiddie treasure box too? Na, I'm just playin' with you. It's cool, especially if you got some candy bars or chips . . . I'm hungry!" says Vince as the class laughs. "You are always hungry, Vince!" shouts another kid from the back.

"Funny you mention that, Vince, because I do have something for that," replies Mr. Jackson with a grin. Glad to see he has captured their interest, he continues, "I have noticed that Chichi's Pizza, just down the street from school, is a hangout for most of you outside of school. So I have worked out a deal with the manager, and I have coupons for free slices that I will be awarding to the best three students of the week. These students must have earned satisfactory progress checks for their Shakespeare assignment, turned in all of their homework assignments, and have no conduct problems or earned any detentions or calls home."

Students are talking among themselves and looking pleased; a few of them even congratulate him on thinking of reaching out to managers at their favorite hangout. Mr. Jackson then asks if there are any questions. As he looks around the room, he notices Joel is not paying attention to the class discussion and is working out of a textbook used in another of his classes. "Joel, you got any questions for me? Perhaps some insight into other ideas I might consider for rewards? Or if you have any questions on the new policy, I would be happy to field those now." Joel mumbles, "Couldn't care less," yet it is still loud enough to be heard by most of the class.

Before Mr. Jackson can respond, Stacey asks in a nasty tone, "Do your old stupid rules still apply, or are they replaced by these newer and stupider rules?" The class falls silent and most eyes are now on Mr. Jackson.

"Actually, Stacey, your question brought up a good point, and I will answer that by saying that, yes, all of the old rules still apply. It is just that now you have these new ones as well. Your question though also demonstrates to the rest of the class how we still are using an old rule in that you just earned a detention for disrespectful behavior. In fact, Stacey, this is your fourth detention, and you have also demonstrated that four detentions earn you a day of in-school suspension." Stacey shrugs her shoulders and puts her head on her desk. Mr. Jackson informs the class that the new rules are in effect and will remain so until the end of the year.

It has been six weeks since the introduction of Mr. Jackson's new class rules, and overall, he has witnessed an increase in engagement and performance with the Shakespeare project. Many students seem to be positively reacting to the bonus points, homework passes, and the pizza coupons, but others seem not to care about the rewards. He wonders if he is not connecting with students.

So he questions some of his choices, and he wonders about considering other ideas for rewards that middle school kids would be more excited about. Maybe a group consequence would help them motivate each other. Although he wonders, how long should he keep this up? Should it be just for this project? Or will students complain and become disinterested during other units that are upcoming? Are there other ways he could help students connect and engage when reading the greats of literature? And he is still unsure whether he has found the best way to deal with the power struggles escalating with Stacey.

Just last week she refused to work with her assigned group and moved her chair to sit with a close friend at another table. When asked to move to her appropriate table, he allowed the back-and-forth to escalate until Stacey was shouting, "I hate you, and I hate this school!" He immediately sent her to the office, but he is unsure how things will progress from this point. He honestly wonders, what are teachers supposed to do when students refuse to listen and follow directions? Stacey stands out in this period, but she is not alone in her defiance. How on earth can he engage these students and get them interested in what he is supposed to be teaching?

DISCUSSION QUESTIONS

1. Classroom Management
   a. Identify this teacher's classroom management strategy and discuss examples that support your answer.
   b. Does this teacher's classroom represent an example of an organized and equitable environment for the students?
   c. Is the behavior modification strategy that Mr. Jackson demonstrates an effective classroom management approach in this case? What are other appropriate management methods for this grade level?
   d. What alternative classroom management models might apply to this case? For example, does Mr. Jackson demonstrate "withitness" in the classroom? If so, how? Is he effective?
   e. Was Mr. Jackson's approach with Stacey effective? Would you classify Mr. Jackson's management strategy in terms of a minor or a moderate intervention?
   f. How serious a concern are classroom management disturbances in middle school? In which grades do teachers most have to prepare for students' disrespect? What about power struggles with students?
   g. How can teachers avoid power struggles with students? How can they most effectively respond to back talk or disrespect from students?

2. Operant Conditioning
   a. Identify the other types of punishments that Mr. Jackson is using. Discuss the role of punishments in a secondary classroom.
   b. Evaluate whether you think Mr. Jackson is using reinforcement/punishment effectively. If not, how could such reinforcers/punishers be used effectively to manage student behaviors?
   c. From the perspective of operant conditioning, what types of continuous reinforcement is Mr. Jackson using? Is Mr. Jackson using any schedules of reinforcement?
   d. Devise other Skinnerian behavior modification techniques that are available to teachers in managing their classrooms.
   e. Summarize the advantages and disadvantages of using applied behavioral analyses as a means for managing behavior in the classroom.

3. Motivation
   a. Is Mr. Jackson's attempt to use extrinsic motivation in this case effective in motivating his students? What negative impact might extrinsic reward systems have on the classroom environment?
   b. Are the external rewards the teacher is employing developmentally appropriate and in tune with the age of his students? What are other types of extrinsic reinforcers that might be of interest to middle school students?
   c. Do you think motivation diminishes as students move from elementary school into middle and high school? Explain how middle and high school teachers can help to motivate their students.
   d. Summarize the importance of increasing intrinsic motivation in the classroom. Explain the methods that Mr. Jackson employs in the case study.
   e. In what ways can the teacher build on strategies for authentic and learning-centered instruction as a way to motivate middle school age students?
   f. How can middle school teachers help students "connect" and see the historical relevance of the literature they are learning about?

4. Adolescent Development
   a. Identify which stage of Piaget's cognitive development students are likely to be in. Support your answer using the case.
   b. Discuss changes in brain development that are occurring during adolescence as they relate to attention, planning, and self-regulation of learning. Is modern technology turning teens into expert multitaskers or making them unable to focus?

c. How can we take some classroom time for the quiet reflection that lets students' minds make connections between past learning and experience and current learning?

d. Do you think students become moodier when they enter adolescence? What biological, psychological, or social forces might influence moodiness?

Case 14

Encounters with Difficult Parents

Suggested Theories: Parent Involvement and Classroom Management
Teacher Challenges: Parent Involvement in the Older Grades and Power
 Struggles with Parents
Student Level: Middle School

Rachel Fuller is getting ready for Parents' Night at the Coast Valley School, a K–8 school where she is a sixth-grade teacher. School has been in session for close to a week, and she is anxious to meet her students' families because she strongly believes that the parent-teacher partnership aids student achievement and behavior. Therefore, she wants to ensure that she and her parents get off on the right foot. She glances around her room, ensuring that all the activities she plans on doing are in the right sequence on her desk and that all the packets of handouts have the correct sheets in them.

Guadalupe Montoya, her Spanish interpreter, peeks her head in the door. "Hi, Guadalupe, please come in." "Hello, Rachel, how are the preparations coming along?" Guadalupe asks. "Oh, great. I was just checking on some last-minute things to avoid getting nervous," Rachel explains. "You will do just fine. It is funny how these nights can still be nerve racking after years of conducting them," Guadalupe answers, and Rachel nods in agreement.

"I have six Hispanic students, but only four of the six will need your interpreting. The other families, I have been assured, are bilingual. Here are their names and the students' names—oh, and please remind them that I will always try to communicate with them through messages in their native language whenever I am able to do so. I explained this to my students and told them to tell their parents, but I would like to ensure they know," Rachel states, handing Guadalupe the list. "Of course, I definitely will. Well, I will make myself at home in the back of the classroom," Guadalupe says as she walks toward the tables set up in the back of the room.

Parents arrive slowly, and as they enter the room and look around they seem unsure of exactly where they should go. "Welcome. Please don't be shy. Come in take a look around, and when you are ready, please take a seat," Rachel states excitedly. Some parents immediately greet Rachel, introduce themselves, briefly identify who they are here for, and move to take a seat. However, Rachel notices that others are choosing to wave to her in greeting but are choosing to stand in groups talking to one another.

It's obvious by their warm greetings that some of these parents know each other; being that some families have been at the school since their children have been in kindergarten it is likely that some of these parents would have formed a close bond. Mindful of the time, Rachel lets parents socialize with each other a little while longer as she answers various brief questions from the flux of incoming parents but then calls out for everyone to please take their seats so they may begin.

Rachel begins the open house by introducing herself, and she discusses what parents can expect their students to learn in her physical science class. She also mentions that this group of students is also her homeroom class. Therefore, she meets with them for fifteen minutes each morning to handle general administrative duties such as school attendance, morning announcements, and important communication with the office.

Once she finishes her introduction, she announces, "Now, I would like the opportunity to get to know you, so if you don't mind, please introduce yourselves and tell us a little something about you and your family. May I have a volunteer to start off?" Rachel asks cheerfully. A parent in the front raises her hand and begins to speak about herself and her son. Before long, all the parents, including the Hispanic parents—with Guadalupe's help—have introduced themselves and spoken of their children and their families. Rachel thanks all the parents and tells them it's wonderful to meet them and that she is excited to have their children in her class this year.

Rachel then says, "Ok, I would like to now discuss some of the class's major assignments to give you all a chance to ask questions," pausing to turn on the computer at her desk and beginning her PowerPoint presentation that is now projected on the whiteboard. "As you can see, I would like to begin by discussing the requirements for the assignments and, in addition, give you a chance to see what some of the completed assignments look like—that is what I am passing around."

Rachel distributes sample assignments to the parents and continues, "Of course, the topics of these assignments are not the same as they were from previous years, but it does nevertheless give you an idea of the length of the assignments, as well as the rigor associated with them." As the parents look down at the materials they are given, Rachel continues her discussion of each assignment as the requirements are projected on the screen on her PowerPoint presentation.

Before continuing, Rachel glances at Guadalupe to verify that the parents seated with her are following along and that she may continue at this pace. Rachel and Guadalupe had discussed prior to Parents' Night that she was to indicate to Rachel with a thumbs-up if she was going at a good pace or a thumbs-down if Rachel needed to slow down to give Guadalupe a chance to catch them up. Rachel gets a thumbs-up from Guadalupe so she knows she can continue. Some parents have raised their hands indicating they have questions, and Rachel then opens the floor to a question-and-answer session on the assignments and requirements.

Rachel then moves the conversation to a discussion of behavior and explains her classroom management strategies. She directs parents to the presentation, which now shows the class rules, and she points to the back of the classroom where the class rules are on a poster. Additionally, she reminds them that both class assignments and class rules can be found on the class's webpage—she has inserted a link in her presentation. Rachel clicks on the link, which takes them all to the class's webpage.

Rachel discusses her expectations for behavior and refers parents to the student handbook that they received from the school about negative consequences for behavior. "Your kids might have already shared with you that I went over what is expected of them in terms of respectful and appropriate classroom behavior, which is so important for this age group. I also discussed in detail what consequences they would have if they broke the rules. Together, we went over examples of how a student could break one of the class rules—especially ones that are more general like disrespect—and then we discussed each consequence. I told them, as I have on my rules sheet, that I will give students one warning for them to control their behavior before I move to a consequence. I do this because even though we are a K–8, the students are now in the middle grades. However, I do expect that all students will abide by the classroom rules and acclimate rapidly."

A parent raises her hand and says, "Ms. Fuller, how do we know if our child is off track? So, for example, do you tell us if they have gotten a warning, or do we find out only when they are in trouble?"

Rachel smiles and says, "That is a great question; it is actually what I was going to discuss next! While I will not be sending daily calendars or agendas for you to sign like you were accustomed to getting throughout elementary school," she pauses and looks around the room as most of the parents nod, "I will, however, send home a monthly progress report with your student that I will need signed. That report lets you know exactly what your child's progress is academically and regarding behavior."

Rachel puts a sample of a blank monthly report on the screen and says, "So as you see here I would indicate whether your child has missing assignments and what your child's grade is on each assignment, and in the box at the bottom I will include behavior. Yes, Guadalupe," Rachel says seeing her hand up. Guadalupe asks, "I have a parent who is asking (signaling to one of the Spanish-speaking parents seated with her) if he would get one and have to sign it even if his child's behavior is fine and his child has no missing assignments?"

Rachel replies, "Yes, all students get a monthly report even if there aren't any problems with behavior or if they're earning good grades. It still needs to be signed, as it lets me know that parents know their student's progress. Most monthly reports will not be blank because I like to include positive comments on the comment box at the bottom of the monthly report—such as sharing something that your child has done that I found to be outstanding." Another parent raises his hand and asks, "What happens if the children don't bring it back signed?"

Rachel answers, "They have three days to return the report before earning a consequence, which is usually having to eat at the quiet table at lunch until the report is returned. If a student neglects to return the monthly report after a week's time, then I will contact you and they will earn a detention." Rachel calls on a parent whose hand was raised in the front, and as the parent begins to speak, he is rudely interrupted by a parent in the back who asks irately, "What about if my kid has misbehaved during that month, but I don't know about it until the monthly report comes out? I mean what would you expect a parent to do if they don't know about it?"

Rachel is taken aback by the parent's demeanor as well as his interrupting what another parent was about to say without any type of apology or even acknowledgment of his interruption. Nonetheless, Rachel answers the parent while mentally noting that she will call on the parent that was interrupted next. "Well, you wouldn't be contacted for a minor infraction because as I said, I first warn the student that they are off task or misbehaving. If the student stops misbehaving, then that is the end of the situation. However, if the student continues to misbehave, then they will have a negative consequence that matches the offense.

"So, for example," she continues, "if the student is working in groups and is being disruptive, then they would have to go back to their seat and complete the work individually. If the student continues to misbehave, then the student would get a detention. Detentions, as is school policy, have an area where the teacher fills out the reason for the punishment, and all detentions need to be signed by a parent. Per school policy, any student who earns more than three detentions in a quarter would have a day of suspension and would need to meet with the teacher. That is different from the K–5 students, so be sure to review your student handbook." The parent doesn't respond, but murmuring is heard from the section of the room where he is seated. Rachel then directs the parents' attention to the bulletin board to the left of the class, telling them that she believes in rewarding accomplishments—there she has listed a series of techniques that she uses for rewarding students for their accomplishments. She also puts a picture of the board magnified on the overhead projector for all to see and then discusses each technique with them. She tells them that way they'll know what their child is talking about when they mention these rewards to them at home.

Rachel then says, "So as you can see I will be celebrating the students' accomplishments, and while of course they have had rewards in elementary school, I try to choose rewards that are in accordance with their age and that the students enjoy. This week we have come up with ideas together of rewards they would like to work toward, and as you can see they are up on that board. I would love for you all to share examples of how you all celebrate accomplishments in your homes." She is pleased to see that Guadalupe has raised her hand indicating that she is going to be translating for one of the parents seated with her.

"Yes, please go ahead," Rachel says as most of the parents turn in their seats to direct their attention to the back of the classroom. "In her home (she motions to the parent sitting immediately to her left), she normally cooks the child's favorite meal and then lets the child choose what the whole family will have for dessert," Guadalupe says. Many of the parents nod in agreement, and some say this is a good idea.

Another parent raises his hand and tells the class that he allows his daughter to skip chores, another informs the class that her son receives an increase in spending money for that week, and finally one mom says she lets her kids choose a special place to go out to eat. A few parents share that they allow their kids to stay up past curfew or give them extra time to spend on their phones, computers, or video games. Rachel sees many parents are turning around complimenting one another's ideas. She is pleased so many parents are volunteering such varied suggestions, and she is thrilled to have a brief look into her students' home life.

Rachel then talks to the parents about how to get involved both in her classroom and in the school—showing them on her class website the area where they can click and see all the upcoming opportunities for them to volunteer in the classroom. Rachel also reminds them that while they are in the same school, they now will be accessing the middle school tab on the main school website for volunteering, as that will give them access not only to general school events but also to events that are specific to the middle grades.

She sees many parents taking note of the changes and hears one parent exclaim that he is happy to hear that she will be encouraging parent involvement in the classroom. He explains that he has not had positive experiences in this regard and that, in his experience, parent involvement is always reduced once a child enters middle school. Rachel agrees that this is a typical view but that her wishes are for parents to increase their involvement in the secondary years because it is fundamental to student learning and achievement. She is a strong advocate of parents being involved in school throughout their children's education.

Rachel feels that this open house was an outrageous success. She had a large turnout and all the parents were receptive, provided her with contact numbers and e-mail addresses, and said to contact them if she ever needed to. Rachel ends with a gift bag she has prepared for each family. The bag contains a magnet that she created out of the list of assignments, due dates, and exam dates as well as tip sheets for the parents and for the students. The tip sheets consist of helpful hints for the student on how to complete each assignment successfully and ideas for the parents on how they can help their children with the assignments.

Many parents personally thank her, letting her know they are delighted to have this type of parent-teacher communication in middle school, and tell her they look forward to meeting her on another occasion. Rachel returns to her computer to load the next class's Parents' Night presentation, but she occasionally looks up to wave goodbye or give brief directions to the parents looking for where their child's next class is. A few parents are lingering behind—one of which is the parent who had yelled out regarding the behavior outcomes. Rachel gets an uneasy feeling as he breaks away from the group and walks toward her.

He introduces himself and his wife, standing next to him, as David's parents. He quickly says, "I want you to explain to me how you gave my son several warnings this week and told him if it hadn't been the first week of school he would have gotten detentions. For what exactly? He said you told him you didn't like the way he talked back to you. What way is that exactly?" Rachel replies, "I expect him to answer respectfully and use a respectful tone . . . as I said to him . . ."

David's mother interrupts her, "What? He's a young boy! I mean he isn't going to talk like an adult! I would think as a teacher you would understand that! I mean that is just ridiculous! How are we supposed to help him with his assignments and keep him on track if we are getting only a monthly report? Can you believe this?" David's mother asks angrily turning to the other parents who remained behind and are watching the exchange. "Tell her, Cynthia, what your daughter said, how she complained about her as well!" David's mother says piercingly as she directs her question at one of the other parents in that group.

The other parent instantly replies infuriated, "Yes, my daughter said she doesn't feel she's going to be able to talk much in your class because you will punish her! All of us in this group and a couple of us are on the School Advisory Committee, and we share the same philosophy for rearing our kids. We encourage self-expression; we want our kids to share their feelings and believe they have a voice. We want them to be able to argue a point if they feel they are right. However, our daughter says that you do not allow that."

She continues, "She said you tell them you are right because you are the teacher and that you don't want to hear anything more about it!" Before Rachel has a chance to respond, David's father interjects angrily, "Oh, so that's it then? If a student questions you too much, then you think he knows more than you about something so you shut him up. If you don't like their opinions, then you punish them? Are you threatened by intelligent students who speak their mind or offer a different opinion than the one you are wanting them to have? We're not putting up with that! We'll see exactly what your principal has to say about all of this!"

DISCUSSION QUESTIONS

1. Parent Involvement and Communication with Difficult Parents
   a. What strengths does the teacher in this case possess regarding parent involvement? Do you see potential weaknesses? If so, how could those weaknesses be strengthened?
   b. The teacher in the case discusses that she sends home a behavior report monthly to be signed by parents. Discuss the effectiveness of this approach in maintaining an open line of communication between parents and teachers. Is the time frame that the teacher has set an appropriate one for students of this age? Why or why not?
   c. In this case, a teacher believed to have done all that she could to prepare for a parents' night is blindsided by parental disrespect toward herself and other parents. Generate ideas for how teachers could most effectively handle a situation such as the one depicted in this case.
   d. Do you feel that the teacher's waiting until the open house to communicate with parents of students who are having behavior problems may have been too late? How may reaching out to the parents earlier regarding student misbehavior have assisted in preventing negative conceptions of the situation and increased the likelihood of more positive teacher-parent communications?
   e. For future conduct problems that this teacher will face in her classroom, what recommendations would you make to the teacher as she

reaches out to communicate to a parent about his or her child's misbehavior via e-mail or phone?

f. Because parent-teacher conferences are likely to result from the problems occurring in this case, what tips for effective parent-teacher conferencing would you offer to this teacher?

g. In this case, the teacher prepares a very organized parents' night for her students' parents. How is that likely to increase parent involvement in her class? Discuss how the teacher informing the parents that she both values parent involvement and feels it is an important component for education factors into those parents' future involvement in the classroom.

h. The teacher in the case uses an interpreter because she knows that some of her students' parents do not understand English. How will that assist her in better communicating with those parents as well as having them feel welcome in her classroom? Discuss the implications that this may have on those students' learning and achievement.

i. This case presents parents who appear to be overinvolved and who came to Parents' Night with a preconceived notion that their child was not at fault for the problems in the class. How can overinvolved parents create discomfort in the learning environment as well as present challenges if volunteering in the class? Discuss ideas for working with overinvolved parents to ensure volunteering in the classroom runs smoothly.

j. How can professional development be geared to helping teachers to handle challenging parents effectively when they are volunteering in the classroom as well as assisting teachers to bridge the gap between students' home and school environments?

2. Classroom Management

a. From what is presented in the case, how would you classify this teacher's classroom management style? Do you feel she is an effective teacher? Why or why not?

b. What reinforcers does the teacher have in place to reward student behavior in her class? What reinforcers are developmentally appropriate for this age group? Which reinforcers would be of interest to older students?

c. Judge the effectiveness of her inviting the parents to share how they reward accomplishments at home. How could having parents share their personal methods increase the likelihood of home-school collaboration?

d. The teacher in this case presents transparency about her assignments and behavior reports, offering parents a look at what assignments should look like, and explains her behavior system and what they are to expect from the behavior reports. Outline other ideas that a teacher could use to ensure parents clearly understand assignments and classroom management procedures in the class.

e. Judge from a parenting standpoint whether it is possible that the concerns that parents brought up in this case about behavior management in this class are valid, given the information that their students are bringing home.

f. It is clear in this case that there are students who began misbehaving at the beginning of the school year. Discuss possible early communication tactics that a teacher can use regarding her classroom management practices when a student starts the year with behavior difficulties. Why would it be beneficial to ensure that the parents have the teacher's side of what has occurred in the classroom as well as their child's?

g. Speculate on what may occur when these parents speak to the principal. What should this teacher be prepared to answer for about her classroom management? Are there any valuable lessons that this teacher can learn from her experience with parents in this class?

3. School Models: Traditional Middle School vs. K–8 Schools
   a. The school that the teacher in this case is instructing at is a K–8 school. As more middle schools consider integrating into a K–8 model, discuss the reasons you believe it could prove beneficial for students' social and academic success. Some research seems to suggest that K–8 schools have fewer behavioral problems and higher academic achievement than traditional middle schools. Speculate as to why this may be the case.
   b. How can removing the transition from elementary to middle school have a positive effect on students' behavior and academics? Why would delaying the transition until the end of their eighth-grade year be beneficial?
   c. From a teacher's perspective, what benefits would K–8 schools have on middle school students' behavior and academic success? Would there be any challenges?

Part VI

INSTRUCTIONAL APPROACHES

Case 15

Making the Most of Academic Learning Time

Suggested Theories: Student-Centered Instruction, Teacher-Centered Instruction, Motivation, and Classroom Climate
Teacher Challenges: Managing Academic Learning Time and Students Who Are Off Task
Student Level: Middle School

Carolina, a sixth grader in Mrs. Romero's fifth-period geometry class at Manchester Academy K–8, cannot wait to begin the day's activities. She knows that Mrs. Romero will get distracted with questions and aiding students with specific problems and she can finish her outline for social studies on the Great Depression, which is due next period. Carolina has figured out that if she can work on her social studies paper during Mrs. Romero's class, she will have it finished by next week and not have to worry about it during the weekend when she wants to spend time with her friends.

Just as Carolina predicted, Mrs. Romero has asked for the students to go about the room and choose the first center to begin working on. Mrs. Romero's class is always structured so that the students have to choose a station to work at during the beginning of the class, and then they complete up to three stations in one period, if time allows. Each station is centered on a specific topic; the current topics are angles and parallel lines, triangles, polygons and polyhedra, circles and spheres, surface area and volume, transformations and symmetry, and geometric inequalities and optimization.

Each station has activities set up that encourage discovery, inquiry, and dialogue. Luckily, Mrs. Romero allows students to work together if they want, and some students pair off with their friends to begin their center's work. Several assignments are prepared to test the students' knowledge in each of the centers, and they each have certain criteria that the students must meet to be considered passing.

Most students immediately find a center they are interested in, but Carolina watches as Josie makes her way to the teacher to ask which center she can go to. Mrs. Romero is fielding a few questions, but patiently reminds Josie it is up to her, although she should choose one she hasn't been to recently. Carolina knows Mrs. Romero is always helpful with the many student questions, and this is one of the reasons she feels confident about doing her homework from another class.

As the period progresses, Carolina feels a huge relief as she finishes her assignment on the Great Depression. She looks at the clock and notices she has a few minutes left in the period. She might be able to get at least one of the center's assignments done. As she makes her way to one, she notices Josie has her hand raised again to ask for the teacher's help. Carolina feels bad for Josie; she is a nice girl but very shy, so she hardly ever works with other students in the class while at the centers.

As Carolina works through her sheet as quickly as possible, she overhears Josie ask for the teacher to look at her work. She wants Mrs. Romero to make sure she is on the right track before she continues. Mrs. Romero stops to help Josie, but Carolina overhears her response, "It's OK, Josie; remember, you just have to make sure you read the instructions carefully, monitor your time accordingly, and leave time to review your answers at the end. I know you can complete these assignments on your own like the rest of the class. However, if you have specific questions or don't understand something, I am happy to help."

At the end of the period, Carolina scribbles off her last answer and heads over to turn it in. She sees Josie has given up on her assignment and put her head down. At that moment, Gracie, one of Carolina's best friends, approaches her after having turned in her work for the day. "What are you doing, girl? That doesn't look like geometry," says Gracie. "Oh, you startled me; I am finishing my social studies outline for next period because it is due and I don't want to be out thirty-five points," answers Carolina as she writes. "Really? Well, what were you doing last night instead of your outline? Isn't that why we got off the phone?" asks Gracie.

"I had every intention of doing it, but then AJ called and you know how that goes; besides, I knew there was always Mrs. Romero's class that I could do it in. Actually, it was AJ who reminded me that he used to do all of his homework in her class and he still earned a B."

"I have to say that is pretty sneaky of you because from afar it always looks like you are doing the work. But aren't you worried that Mrs. Romero will notice that you did not turn in any of the centers' assignments?" inquires Gracie frowning. "Nah, Mrs. Romero is so easygoing that I just tell her I forgot to turn in my work, and she'll accept it tomorrow, when I have had a chance to read Reese's notes in seventh period; I mean she is such a brain!" answers

Carolina casually as both girls pack up their belongings and await the bell that signals they may go to lunch.

The bell rings and they both head toward their lockers before going to lunch. As the girls walk, Gracie continues the conversation about Mrs. Romero's centers. "I just can't believe that the information on the centers doesn't interest you any. I mean some of the way that this work is set up is pretty cool. And it is nice that Mrs. Romero is not always drilling us for information or having us sit there doing seat work like Mr. Bernard does in social studies. I mean she hardly even gives us any homework, and even when she does it is always applying things, which I happen to think is kinda fun . . . for schoolwork.

"However," she continues, "you know what I have a problem with? I am tired of Samuel and Michaela always copying my assignment sheets. Half the time they aren't even talking about geometry, which is a huge distraction when I am trying to figure the stuff out! Then, they just assume I'm going to let them use all my answers. They do it all the time, and Mrs. Romero just gives them the same grade and never says boo about it." Carolina is frowning, but before she can say anything, one of their friends in another class walks up.

"What's up, ladies?" Leroy asks as he slips his arms around both girls who are closing their lockers. "Hi, Leroy. Gracie and I were just talking about Mrs. Romero's class and heading off to lunch."

"Great, wait for me to put these books in my locker and I will walk with you," Leroy says happily as both girls nod and pause to wait for their friend.

In the cafeteria, Carolina, Gracie, and Leroy join a few more of their friends who have already begun eating. "So, Carolina, were you able to do the outline for social studies?" asks AJ taking a bite of his sandwich. "Oh, yeah, it was no problem," replies Carolina. "You must be talking about Mrs. Romero's class," announces Leroy taking a sip of his drink as he continues. "I swear, me and AJ, well actually a lot of us, must have done all of our other work in there last year and we all passed. I don't think she ever had a clue. It is a shame more classes aren't like hers."

Deanna, one of the other students seated at the table says, "I like Mrs. Romero though; she is such a sweetheart and so knowledgeable. I think the way she sets up her class makes the time go by so fast you don't even feel like you are there to learn. Well, I guess for those of us who are actually doing the assignments and learning that is." She pauses to wink at AJ and Leroy and continues, "I mean if I have to sit through another period in Ms. Ellis's English class, I will just scream!" Deanna exclaims dramatically and continues. "I mean we never get to express our opinions; she just lectures, lectures, lectures, and expects us to just listen for the whole hour. Ugh, it is so frustrating."

"Oh, tell me about it . . . and what about Mr. Bernard's class?" Gracie asks not pausing long enough to warrant a reply as she continues, "he has that question-and answer-session, you all know, the one where he gives you about two seconds to answer a question and then he is off to another student."

"Yeah, and then he takes away points from your grade for not knowing the answer," Leroy interjects while eating. "I remember that guy; he is a tool!" Leroy finishes. The group of students all nod their heads at Leroy in agreement.

Carolina adds, "And I hate how you never know what information Mr. Bernard will ask on the test because his lessons are all over the place; it is like he never knows what he is teaching so it makes it soooo confusing. Not to mention he always acts like he does not want to be here, like he is always bored with us or something." All the students nod their heads in agreement. "Well, I heard that he is getting out of teaching because he is burned out . . . that is what Coach Wilkins told us, right Leroy?" asks AJ looking for confirmation from his friend. "Yeah, that's right! I guess most of our teachers just stink," Leroy answers as he peels a banana.

"Oh, c'mon, man, they are not all that bad; Mr. Kim is alright," says Phinn, who until now had been too busy eating to add to his friends' comments. Phinn continues, "I mean Mr. Kim talks too, you know, but he has good review sessions that you can pay attention to if you missed something the day before. What does he call them?" Phinn asks as he pauses. "Mind refreshers because they are supposed to refresh your mind from the day before," Carolina answers and continues, "I am sure they come in handy, Phinn, especially when you miss something in class because you are too busy drooling over Miranda!"

The students all laugh, including Phinn, who adds, "Well, it's because she is cool and really pretty, and in Mr. Kim's class, we have a chance to work in groups. I mean how fresh would that be if she and I get to be in the same group?" Phinn smiles at his male counterparts, who agree with Phinn, while the female students laugh and roll their eyes.

Gracie adds while jokingly tapping Phinn on the forearm, "And lucky for you then that Mr. Kim also reviews at the end, so people like you can make sure they got all of the right answers." AJ says, "Today, though we did something like Mrs. Romero's class, you know with centers. But unlike Mrs. Romero's class, things are better coordinated and you definitely have to do the work or you get an F for the day." At that point, the bell rings indicating lunch has ended and all of the students make their way to their next class of the day.

DISCUSSION QUESTIONS

1. Teacher-Centered Instruction
   a. Discuss the planning methods when preparing teacher-centered instruction.

b. Explain the approaches that are characteristically associated with teacher-centered instruction.

c. Identify the characteristics of teacher-centered instruction. Which teachers in the case study are using teacher-centered approaches to instruction as described by their students?

d. Summarize how wait time regarding questioning affects student learning. Describe how questioning can be used effectively. Integrate examples from the case.

e. Outline the potential benefits of using teacher-centered instruction. Diagram what techniques increase the effectiveness of teacher-centered instruction. Explain how these techniques were demonstrated in the case.

f. Discuss the criticisms for teacher-centered instruction, in particular direct instruction. How is this demonstrated in this case?

g. Explain the role of taxonomies of educational objectives in planning.

2. Student-Centered Instruction

a. Compare how the planning methods for student-centered instruction differ from those of teacher-centered instruction. Discuss the role of objectives in learner-centered instruction.

b. Which teachers in the case study are using student-centered approaches to instruction as described by their students? Explain the potential benefits of using student-centered instruction. Cite examples from the case.

c. Discuss how Mrs. Romero may have made errors in the way that she conducted her lessons. How may her teaching approach be made more effective in reaching all students?

d. How has the teacher's use of guided discovery gone off track in this case? Discuss ways the teacher could more effectively structure her opportunities for guided discovery.

e. Discuss how problem-based or authentic learning could be incorporated into math classes. What implications will this have for students' academic engagement?

f. Did Mrs. Romero use cooperative learning effectively? What tips would you offer should this teacher want to implement more structured cooperative learning during her learning centers? Do you think it is wise for teachers to allow students to choose who they work with during cooperative learning? What might be better ways to group students?

g. What concerns are raised in this case about individual accountability when students work cooperatively? What strategies might a teacher employ to ensure all students are accountable for the work?

h. Outline additional teaching methods not used in this case that are consistent with student-centered instruction.

i. What special challenges does a student like Josie pose? Do some students struggle with more independent learning? How can teachers encourage students to work independently? How might some strategies in encouraging students' self-regulated learning be helpful here?

j. Describe potential problems for designing student-centered instruction.

3. Motivation

a. What is academic learning time (ALT)? What steps can teachers take to ensure a productive use of ALT in their classrooms?

b. Do you see evidence of students being intrinsically or extrinsically motivated in this case? How can a teacher effectively balance each?

c. How can teachers ensure their students are engaged in appropriate class activities that are not teacher directed?

d. How can educators help students to manage their time and work independently on assignments in the classroom?

e. How can teachers use learning centers for differentiated instruction and adaptive teaching that engages students by building on their strengths?

f. Discuss the general characteristics of effective or good teaching.

g. Explain the teachers in the cases that the students find effective, and discuss what methods they may be employing that account for their success.

4. Classroom Climate

a. Do you feel Mrs. Romero has created a productive classroom climate? Why or why not? Do you feel she has adequate classroom organization? Instructional support?

b. Do you feel this teacher has created a proper balance between teacher and student-centered instruction?

c. How can an effective classroom management approach help to minimize students' off-task behavior?

d. What classroom management recommendations might you make for Mrs. Romero?

e. Does Mrs. Romero demonstrate "withitness" in the classroom? Do you think she does an adequate job maintaining academic momentum in her classroom? What strategies would you offer for optimizing her "withitness"?

f. How might classroom routines be beneficial for classroom learning?

g. What questions should teachers consider when designing learning spaces in the classroom in order to maximize student learning?

Case 16

Meaningful Authentic Learning

Finding the Funding

Suggested Theories: Learner-Centered Instruction, Situated Learning, Authentic
   Instruction and Assessment, and Performance Assessment
Teacher Challenges: Creating Effective and Authentic Learning Opportunities,
   Matching Instruction to Assessment, and Funding Opportunities
Grade Level: High School

Ms. Gillespie's tenth-grade American history students are very excited as
they walk back to their classroom from lunch today. That's because today is
the long-awaited opening of Gillespie's Shoppe! Gillespie's Shoppe is not an
actual store but rather a stage-like theater that Ms. Gillespie sets up in her
classroom, and she teaches an entire unit centered around colonial America
for which her classroom is turned into a picturesque scene from those times.

Ms. Gillespie's students engage in various projects, presentations, and
performances that serve to demonstrate their knowledge of the information in
the unit. Ms. Gillespie is known for her unique projects, which allow students
to be engaged with different learning approaches and on different levels. She
also believes in assessing students both traditionally and alternatively using
unit tests based on the book chapters but also portfolios, summaries, presentation reports, live exhibitions, and peer evaluations.

Gillespie Shoppe is a concept that all the students have taken part in and
have helped construct for the past few weeks. Ms. Gillespie smiles as she
surveys the classroom now turned into The Shoppe, as some of her students
have nicknamed it, and is thrilled with the fruits of their labor. Ms. Gillespie
knows that she is very fortunate to have generous donations via her Go Fund
Me page, where parents and relatives of her students have been giving money
to the project for months and helping make all this possible.

Because Ms. Gillespie is a good seamstress, she enjoys being able to sew costumes that resembled the appropriate attire for the times, which she feels gives the students a chance to fully experience an entirely different way of life. Ms. Gillespie's husband majored in the fine arts, and her sister is handy with tools; thus they are always happy to lend her a hand with artistic depictions as well as construction of the set.

Gillespie's Shoppe is quite an undertaking, and Ms. Gillespie is always thankful for her family's assistance as well as the monetary donations from parents. She knows otherwise, she wouldn't be able to engage in this and other educational projects she does throughout the year since locating funding for projects is not always easy and budgetary constraints pose limitations for educators' choice of activities.

She wanted to have her students experience real-life situations based on a store in which they could employ the concepts they are learning in the classroom. The Shoppe is unique in that it represents colonial America, and the store, its visitors, and owners will experience for a brief time what living life in that era would have been like. Ms. Gillespie immerses both herself and her students in this project, giving them various tasks prior to the onset of The Shoppe that count toward one of the students' assignments.

Students created various aspects of the store out of construction paper, paper, construction foam, and poster board, being careful to ensure that their creations matched the rubric's descriptions of life in those times. Additionally, every student in the class plays a role in the store, as each student is assigned to a family or is a single character with real-life problems they must resolve that were typical of the times. Ms. Gillespie researched the problems to ensure they would have traditionally been encountered in colonial America, and then she created learning situations that students could investigate and resolve according to those times.

Ms. Gillespie based each of the problems that students must resolve on general domains: currency, customs, education, medicine, religion, and transportation. Each family of students was given two problems to explore and for which they must create a portfolio that depicts their resolutions as well as make a presentation in which they introduce their family, its background and challenges, as well as their proposed solutions. Ms. Gillespie grades everything on a rubric that she gives the students along with the initial instruction for each assignment so that the students know exactly how they will be assessed.

A few of Ms. Gillespie's students are walking back from lunch discussing excitedly how much they are looking forward to the opening of The Shoppe. As they reach their lockers, Bailee says animatedly, "Seriously, how excited are you all for The Shoppe to open?" Her friends all agree, and Keira replies, "It's awesome that this is our class for the next few weeks! What a nice change from all our other classes. And all the work we have been doing is finally going to pay off. Have you all been working well in your groups, or I mean families?"

The girls all nod, and Natasha, who just joined the group, says, "Oh yeah! We've been working well outside of class; when we can't meet at one of our houses then we do the group part of the assignment through video chat. You know, I was a little hesitant at first because our groups are so . . . well . . . different. I mean I have kids in my groups that I've never even talked to before this project. But it's worked out great!" The rest of the group agrees that the work hasn't been challenging and has been fun. They all like that while they get a grade for their group work, they also have portions of the assignment they are responsible for on their own.

"I'm excited to see what costumes Ms. Gillespie came up with!" exclaims Amelia. "I know, she is so creative! You know, so many people I have talked to are so jealous that we have Ms. Gillespie because few of the other teachers take teaching to this level!" exclaims Keira. "And because Ms. Gillespie is cool she isn't going to dress us up like dorks! I mean that would be a tragedy! I mean I don't mind playing the role as long as I look good playing it!"

The girls all agree, and Bailee says, "You know, the weird thing is normally at this time of the year I have gymnastics on the brain since my mom and I are always traveling with my gymnastics team, and when I saw all the research I had to do for this I was like whoa! But I actually found myself getting into it—I mean my character, you know, is in love with a boy whose family is in a feud with mine. So although we are in love, we cannot marry, and actually, I am promised to marry this man who is, like, thirty years older than me! Ah no! Can you even imagine that?"

The girls share their disbelief, and Amelia adds, "I mean can you imagine living in a time in which women were given off in marriage to whomever their father chose? That is insane. My dad would choose a nerdy guy for me—I'd hate it!" They all giggle and list who they think their fathers would choose. Bailee then says, "Actually, OK, so be ready to freak out! You know the section of the assignment where we had to research how one of our colonial problems could tie into our society today? Well, I learned all about arranged marriages and how there are societies that still practice this today." Keira exclaims incredulously, "You're not serious! Where is that?"

Bailee smiles and says proudly, "Well, my friends, you are about to find out when my group goes on Friday! I wouldn't want to spoil the surprise!" The girls laugh and try to hurry Keira up, who is trying to freshen up her makeup in her locker mirror. "Hmm, c'mon lipstick girl! We're going to be late!" Bailee says playfully, while Kiera turns around to ask her friend's opinion on her choice of lipstick color. "Yeah, it looks great! Is it new?" Amelia asks. "Yes, I just got it! I wanted a new shade! Let's remember who my colonial husband is; I mean, is he hot or what? And unlike you all I am single and would very much like his attention!"

The girls all laugh agreeing. As they walk toward the classroom, Bailee suddenly stops and says, "You all don't think that Ms. Gillespie would make us take our makeup off do you? I mean, they did not use it back then!" Ms. Gillespie who is standing at the door to her classroom overhears her students and decides to interject to put their minds at ease. "Now, ladies, I would not do that. My goal is not to interfere with your social lives or to make you uncomfortable, but rather to teach you a thing or two about history."

All of them laugh, and as they enter the classroom the students are transported back in time. All of the desks have been moved to the front of the class, and the room has been converted into a storefront and actual store. A sign that reads "The Gillespie Shoppe" in black letters hangs on top of the door the students created. On the wall closest to the classroom entrance hangs a bulletin board that explains what the Gillespie Shoppe is, what it is for, and which learning units are associated with this assignment. The students are all standing around admiring their work and discussing The Shoppe when the bell rings indicating class has begun.

"All right, everyone, please listen," says Ms. Gillespie loudly. "I know today you are all trying to take it all in and I understand that. However, shortly we do need to get moving on our presentations. You are all aware of which days you present; according to my list, the Windsor family presents today along with the Calvert family. The students belonging to those families as well as The Shoppe owners need to go over to the costume area, find their names, and please put the costumes on."

"The rest of you, please pick up a grading sheet that as you all know will serve as the peer evaluation part of your assignments. Remember, be clear with your comments since you all will be helping me assess your classmates on their performances." All the students hurriedly assume their roles, and soon the class is transported back in time.

Ms. Gillespie later reflects on the successful first week of The Shoppe. She is thrilled that her students are enjoying the projects and have certainly done a fantastic job collaborating! The group portfolios she has graded have proven to exhibit a high caliber of achievement.

However, a sense of unease fills her as she sees the e-mail from the administration regarding the upcoming state testing. Seeing that the timing of the test coincides with her unit on The Shoppe, there will not be much time for her to review concepts before her students take the standardized tests. Ms. Gillespie hopes that she has prepared them enough to do well. While her students do very well on the alternative assessments she has given them on this unit on The Shoppe, she does worry that the knowledge will not generalize to the more traditional school-wide state assessments.

DISCUSSION QUESTIONS

1. Social Constructivism
   a. Discuss the theory of situated cognition. How does this case support its claims?
   b. How does the teacher use authentic instruction in this case? Is her instruction effective? Why or why not? Generate ideas for other ways in which teachers can use authentic instruction in the classroom.
   c. Compare the necessary planning that authentic instruction and traditional instruction would require. Has this teacher planned well for The Shoppe? Explain your answer.
   d. The teacher in the case is using elements of problem-based learning. Discuss the advantages that this type of instructional strategy has for students' learning and achievement.
   e. Discuss the teacher's use of cooperative learning. Identify key aspects of cooperative learning that are apparent in the case. What key elements of cooperative learning should always be present when constructing the group? What about other ingredients that are important for cooperative learning to be effective?
   f. Is the teacher in this case helping to construct a community of learners? If so, how is she achieving this result? If not, how could she achieve it?
   g. What is guided discovery learning? Do you see elements of it in this case? What are important tips for structuring guided discovery successfully? How can teachers sufficiently guide the experience so that students proceed toward covering important standards and learning objectives?
   h. Is the instruction used in this case leading to successful learning? Is this type of learning likely to generalize to state testing? Why or why not?
   i. How do teachers respond to, or handle, any erroneous or incorrect conclusions students arrive at during student-centered instruction?

2. Assessment and Instruction
   a. What relationship exists between assessment and instruction? Why is this relationship important for teachers?
   b. Identify the various types of assessments that the teacher in this case is using. Is she using them all effectively?
   c. Is the performance assessment portion of The Shoppe carried out effectively? Discuss the benefits that this type of approach has for students' learning. Disadvantages?
   d. The teacher uses peer evaluations in this case. What advantages and disadvantages are there with the use of peer evaluations?
   e. Discuss how the instructional approach the teacher is using in this case may or may not be directly linked to the upcoming state assessments

she refers to at the end of the case. What problems does this present for teachers? How does the push for accountability impact teachers and students? Should assessments be linked to the type of material that teachers are instructing on?

   f. Discuss the benefits of teachers using both formative and summative assessments in the classroom. Do you think each purpose of assessment is being adequately considered in this case?

3. Challenges with Funding Opportunities and Effective Authentic Instruction
   a. The teacher in this case states that she has had external assistance with funding this project via an online class page. What other ideas can you generate for teachers to gain financial assistance for class projects?
   b. What difficulties can teachers encounter when asking parents for funding?
   c. How can students' socioeconomic levels affect a teacher's ability to ask parents for monetary support? Generate ideas for other ways parents can contribute to such projects that don't involve donating money.
   d. Outline limitations that lack of funding could place on a teacher's being able to create effective authentic learning opportunities in the classroom.
   e. Identify and discuss the time demands that using authentic instruction may place on the teacher. How could that deter some teachers from engaging in this type of instruction?
   f. How could teachers who lack the ability to conduct projects due to low resources or lack of time affect their students' exposure to innovative learning techniques?

4. Adolescent Social Development
   a. Identify which of Erikson's stages of psychosocial development the students are likely to be functioning in. Support your answer using examples from the case.
   b. How is the crisis typical of this stage of Erikson's psychosocial development demonstrated in the students' interactions in this case?
   c. Discuss Elkind's adolescent egocentrism. How is it apparent in this case?
   d. In general, how is identity formed and self-concept developed? How can this teacher's approach to instruction help students with these developmental tasks?
   e. Apply Marcia's theory of identity formation to this case. How would adolescent relationships and friendships affect their performances in projects such as the one discussed in this case?

Part VII

ASSESSMENT AND EVALUATION

Case 17

Meaningful and Fair

Grading Subjective Assessments

Suggested Theories: Alternative and Traditional Assessment, Authentic
 Assessment, and Fair Teaching Practices
Teacher Challenges: Grading Subjective Classroom Assessment, Students
 Arguing about Grades, Teacher Favoritism, Parental Complaints about
 Grading, and Student-Directed Learning
Grade Level: High School

"OK, now we are talking," Bobby Pritchard exhaled. Mr. Pritchard is a
tenured teacher at Middleston Heights High School with a wealth of teaching experience under his belt. During this long teaching campaign, he has
become bored and disillusioned with the preponderance of traditional types
of classroom assessment.

In this final week before the start of the new school year, he has put the final
touches on his new major classroom assessment method of an E-portfolio, an
electronic project that would catalogue his tenth graders' mastery of world
history. He gives one more cursory glance to his instructional handout on
the project that outlined each of the major sections of the portfolio: Ancient
Egypt, Greeks and Romans, Medieval Europe, Renaissance and Reformation,
and two final sections on student self-reflection and resources for continued
learning.

It is the first day of class, and Mr. Pritchard has just introduced the portfolio
project. "So, class, this will represent 75 percent of your grade in the class.
You will still have some tests, but most of your grade will come from the
grades you receive on the portfolio due at intermittent times during the term
as outlined on your handout. Now, I want to give you a real idea of the materials that might be included in your portfolio. Really expand your thinking on
how to demonstrate your mastery!"

"For instance, you might include written essays, concept maps, charts and tables, significant newspaper and magazine clippings, and video/audio recordings of any performance exercises you put together. And you will be able to upload your files into a cloud storage account." A couple of students, Brent and Samuel, seem excited about the electronic nature of the assignment. However, Charlotte, one of his more perfectionist students, raises her hand to say, "But, Mr. Pritchard, what's this about the last two portfolio sections on self-reflection and resources?"

"Good question," Mr. Pritchard responds while addressing the class at large. "In the self-reflection section I want you to chart your learning progress. Perhaps you could include some journal or self-analysis entries that list stumbling blocks and how you overcame then. Then, in the final section on resources for continued learning, you might keep a running catalog of books, journals, magazines, e-mail contacts, websites, or other helpful resources as you continue your journey in learning our country's history."

He continues, "I really think everyone will take a great deal more from their learning after this project. Instead of just memorizing some isolated facts, albeit documenting some great points in history, now you will have the opportunity to engage in critical thinking and problem solving about these issues! Think how much more meaningful this will be than some boring old pencil-and-paper tests. This way, you will be using state-of-the art word processing and graphics available in the classroom or through your own personal use at home!"

At this point, Charlotte raises her hand again. As Mr. Pritchard inwardly rolls his eyes, he calls on Charlotte. "But, Mr. Pritchard, how will we be graded on this?" The teacher pauses for a moment and notices that Charlotte has now managed to capture the entire class's collective attention, a feat most teachers would envy.

He responds, "Why, Charlotte, just like any other paper or project would be graded. What I will do is pick out those portfolios that truly represent the best products and use them as samples in which to grade the remaining class projects. I will be looking for each section to have documentation using a diverse sampling of materials. But that is another good question, Charlotte. Maybe what I should do is work on a supplementary handout that will list some criteria before the first upcoming deadline."

A few students look skeptical at this point, but most nod their heads and look to the teacher for the next step on the day's agenda. He asks Brent and his group to begin the slide presentation they have been working on. He has been following their work and knows it will make a great segue to get students focused on the day's instruction.

It is the end of the second week of school, and by the end of the third week the students would be submitting their portfolios for the first time. Mr. Pritchard is on his way home for the day when he stops in for his messages in the main office of the school. He is surprised to see two slips from concerned parents, including Charlotte Jones's mother. He steps into the faculty lounge to return the calls. Since he has met Mrs. Jones before, a mother very much involved with the school's advisory council, he calls her first.

"Hi, Mrs. Jones, this is Mr. Pritchard from Middleston returning your call. What can I do you for?" Mrs. Jones replies, "Oh hi, Bobby, please call me Lily. We don't need to stand on formalities; I feel like I know you so well already. But, I am glad you called. I was just a bit concerned about this portfolio assignment. Charlotte expressed to me how much of their grade it represented. And, well, when she has been struggling with the project the past few nights, I became concerned that Charlotte was so frustrated and that the project weighed so much, especially since they really didn't know what exactly you wanted."

Mr. Pritchard communicates his appreciation for alerting him of her concerns and shares how he has promised to put together a criteria handout. Unfortunately, it had completely slipped his mind given this first trial run smoothing out all the other administrative tasks associated with the project. Lily immediately jumps in saying, "That was another thing; I have always heard you to be a fair teacher, so it surprised me when you made such a new project worth so much of their grade in the class. Seems there should have been more of a transition period."

"I also wondered about the more traditional types of assessment," the mother continues. "Charlotte is such a stellar test taker as you know! It doesn't seem quite fair that their grade pretty much rides on this project. I see the good points about the project, but while schooling should be about learning to think and solve problems, it is also about gaining the basic content knowledge so they are prepared for college as well, right?" Mr. Pritchard hesitates and decides he needs to regroup given Mrs. Jones's comments. So he politely promises to look into the issue and get back to her the following week.

Mr. Pritchard glances at the second call slip wondering what parent complaints it heralds. Given his years in the field, he knows that parent communication usually means one thing, parental dissatisfaction. After he returns the second call, he realizes he was right. Mrs. Franklin, Richard's mother, is concerned because she feels her son will be at a disadvantage because while he has a computer it is not a new one and it only has basic word processing. In addition, they do not have Wi-Fi at home, so he may not have the same multimedia displays that other students have with newer computers with the latest software.

Mrs. Franklin wants assurances that her son won't be penalized unfairly. She is also concerned where all Richard's work will be stored and who will have access. Will others not in the class be able to view the work? Will it be out "on the Internet" for others to see? After assuring Richard's mother he will consider her concerns as well as providing some contact information for local public libraries with free computing, the teacher hangs up in weary defeat. He groans as he heads out the door. He realizes all will look better now that the weekend is here.

A couple of weeks later, Mr. Pritchard reflects on his first round of grading of the E-portfolio between classes. He concedes the new project has led to a much greater percentage of his time than expected. And while he knows the learning outcomes will pay out in the end, there were many things he didn't prepare for. But he hopes the criteria sheet he had drafted and shared was a help. Many students seemed to do well, and they put together a nice synopsis of their learning. Yet others didn't fare as well. Michael's portfolio appears to be hastily prepared and doesn't seem to show any substantive learning.

However, he knows Michael's grades on other homework assignments may be reflecting a lack of time management and willingness to follow through on his schoolwork. So he is worried about his independent study habits. When he tried to talk to him quietly in class while students were doing group work, he offered a series of excuses about other things he had going on, being able to get enough time to pull everything together, and not being sure what he wanted anyway. He is not sure if it's a motivational issue or Michael truly struggles with setting and managing goals for such a large project.

Then there is Charlotte. Charlotte is very bright and performs at the top of the class. But she didn't do as good job as other students in being able to catalog her learning with a range of examples to document her learning. And she only seemed willing to include excellent work while not documenting learning improvement over time. Her self-assessments lacked any reference to what learning goals could be improved over time.

At this point Charlotte storms into the classroom, showing up early for class. "Mr. Pritchard, I saw my folio grade online, and I don't understand why you only gave me a B+. I did what you said. I included some of the examples you told us to. It doesn't seem fair that Brent gets an A for doing the same level of work that I did! Just because he is on the football team it seems he gets easier treatment than some of the rest of us." Mr. Pritchard pauses a moment and makes a concerted effort to remain composed in the face of Charlotte's anger.

He calmly replies, "I can see that you are disappointed with your grade, and I am more than happy to sit down and discuss your project, the criteria, and how you can improve . . ." Before he can explain, Charlotte interjects, "That's just it. How can you justify my grade against criteria that weren't clear, that we got late, and only after I had already almost completed my portfolio? I will tell you my mom is on my side on this. She's still waiting to hear from you, so I know you're gonna hear from her."

"And I am not the only one. Other students are angry too! I talked to some of my friends in other classes with big projects, and they got a rubric from the start with clear guidelines to follow. How are we supposed to know how we are going to be graded when you don't even appear to know? On top of that, it counts so much for our grade in the class!"

Seeing some of the looks that their conversation is getting them from the students as they file into the class, Mr. Pritchard makes a couple more attempts to calm Charlotte down, but she isn't having any of it. Charlotte storms over to her seat in the class and gets on her phone while shooting looks over to the teacher as the bell rings. Mr. Pritchard isn't sure how he will manage to pull off a smooth lesson this period, and he also worries about what voice mail he will soon have coming from Charlotte's mother.

DISCUSSION QUESTIONS

1. Portfolio Assessment
   a. Distinguish between process and best works portfolios. Which does the teacher in this case seem to be using? How could his method be revised into the other type of portfolio assessment?
   b. Compare and contrast how the two uses of portfolios relate to the notion of formative vs. summative evaluation.
   c. An effective tip for using portfolio assessment is to involve students in selecting the pieces that will make up the portfolio. How might Mr. Pritchard have better allowed for this bit of advice?
   d. Evaluate the strengths and weaknesses of the teacher's use of the portfolio exercise. In general, what are the merits of portfolio assessment? Limitations?
   e. In what ways could the portfolio assessment have been more effectively planned and implemented?
   f. How might a scoring rubric have helped in this case? Create an example for a rubric that would work in this case.
   g. How can teachers ensure portfolio assessments align with important curricular objectives and state standards?
   h. What role can self-reflection or self-assessment play in portfolio usage? What are examples of student artifacts that include self-reflection? How can self-reflection elements be used most effectively to encourage student learning?
   i. Which event in the case do you see relating to self-regulated learning? What role might goal setting play within self-regulation? How can teachers use self-assessment activities to encourage students' adaptive learning strategies? How might teachers encourage students' self-regulatory skills? How can homework be used as a vehicle to practice these skills?
   j. Discuss whether a physical or electronic portfolio format is more suitable depending on the circumstances.

  k. What challenges do electronic portfolios create in terms of storage, access, and privacy of students' work?

2. Alternative vs. Traditional Assessment
  a. What makes an assessment authentic or alternative?
  b. Analyze the issues of reliability and validity of traditional vs. alternative assessment.
  c. Evaluate the following argument: "Traditional tests are a poor basis for classroom assessment."
  d. How can the teacher in this case more effectively balance traditional and alternative types of assessment in his classroom?
  e. In what ways can teachers ensure that grades for alternative types of assessment are still based on objective evidence of student learning?
  f. Discuss whether you will use authentic assessment approaches like portfolios and performance exhibitions in your own teaching.

3. Traditional Tests and Question Types
  a. Identify the merits of traditional testing.
  b. Describe types of traditional testing the teacher might use in his classroom.
  c. Provide some guidelines for constructing traditional tests. What are important ideas to remember when creating true-false, multiple-choice, and matching items?
  d. Identify some uses of computers in assessment. How confident do you currently feel about being able to use computers for assessment? What do you need to learn?

4. Fair Testing Practices
  a. Identify opportunities for bias in grading. How can teachers guard against bias in grading?
  b. In particular, how can teachers guard against favoritism influencing their evaluation of students?
  c. How can teachers demystify the criteria for success on an alternative assessment?
  d. Evaluate Mr. Pritchard's explanation of grading policies to students. Were his explanations and standards reasonable?
  e. How will you explain your grading system to parents? How can communication with families support students' learning?
  f. If you were Mr. Pritchard, how would you proceed given students' and teachers' legitimate concerns with the portfolio project? In what ways can this teacher improve his communication with parents over their legitimate concerns with his assessment practices?

Index

middle school Parents' Night
and, 113–21; questions on middle
school, 120–21; questions related
to cell phone distractions and, 57;
questions related to disrespect
and, 110; questions related to
parental communications and,
120, 121; questions related
to special learning challenges
and, 49; questions related to
technology use and, 104; role
of teacher and, 97–106; seating
style, 54, 57; teacher "withitness"
and, 104, 110, 130
cognitive development theories: in
academic honesty case, 17–23;
in adolescent relationships and
social media influence, 59–65;
cyberbullying and, 25–31; Internet
plagiarism case and, 11–15;
questions related to adolescent
cliques and, 7; questions related
to adolescent relationships and,
64–65; questions related to
cyberbullying and adolescent
identity, 30; questions related
to grade complaints and, 73–74;
questions related to Internet
plagiarism and, 14–15; questions
related to middle school academic
honesty and, 22; questions related
to role of teacher and, 106; role
of teacher and, 97–106; rumor
spreading through social media
and, 64. *See also* metacognition;
social cognitive theory
college: gender and, 40; preparing for,
90; pressure of choosing and
applying to, 88, 89, 90
communication: parental, 81–85,
119–21; questions on difficult
parents and, 119–20
community service learning project,
91–92
compulsive texting, social development
and, 58

concept mapping, 69, 73
contraceptive pill, 26
cooperative learning, 7; geometry class
activity centers, 125–26, 128
cyberbullying: adolescent identity and,
25–31; suggested theories for, 25

disabilities. *See* learning disabilities
disruptions, student, 81–85

educational technology, Internet
plagiarism and, 11–15
engine analogy, 89, 92
English, math student disinterest in, 108
English literature class, high school,
adolescent cliques case, 3–9
environmental science class, Internet
plagiarism in, 11–14
equitable teaching practices: gender
equity in science case study,
35–43; questions related to gender
equity and, 43
Exceptional Student Education (ESE),
middle school case study
involving, 45–49

fair teaching practices, world history
class portfolios and, 139–44
fair testing practices, questions related
to portfolios and, 144
friendships, student-teacher, high
school psychology class and,
97–106
funding: for authentic instruction, 131,
132, 136; questions related to,
136

gender: group projects and, 38–39; math
self-efficacy and, 84; science
programs and, 40
gender differences and stereotypes:
gender equity in science case,
35–43; questions related to, 42
gender equity: case study, 35–43;
equitable teaching practices
and, 43; suggested theories and

learned helplessness theory, girls'
confidence in math and, 81–85
learner-centered instruction. *See*
student-centered instruction
Learner-Centered Psychological
Principles, xi
learner differences, INTASC Model
Core Teaching Standards link to,
xii
learning: cooperative, 125–26, 128;
INTASC standard link to,
xii; making time for, 125–30;
problem-based, 135; self-
regulated, 67–77, 87–94; situated,
131–36
learning and instruction theories:
learning disabilities and, 45–49;
questions on individual and
multimodal, 48–49. *See also*
observational learning theories;
self-regulated learning
learning challenges, middle school
language arts class, 45–49
learning disabilities: middle school
language arts class case, 45–49;
questions related to, 48; questions
related to grade complaints and,
75, 76
learning strategies: community service
project and, 91–92; grade
complaints and ineffective study
skills case, 67–77; questions
related to disinterested students
and, 74–75
life science class, tenth-grade, gender
equity case study, 35–43
literature and composition class, cell
phone distraction in middle
school, 53–58
literature class: in adolescent cliques
case study, 3–9; back talk
problem in middle school, 107–12

math: questions related to self-efficacy
and, 83–84, 92; stress in high
school, 87–94

memory: question related to role of
attention in, 74; questions related
to ineffective study skills and,
73–74
metacognition: grade complaints and
ineffective study skills case,
67–77; questions related to, 75
middle school case studies: academic
honesty, 17–23; back talk
problem, 107–12; cell phones
in class, 53–58; complaining
about grades, 67–77; ESE issues
in middle school language arts
class, 45–49; girls needing
encouragement in algebra
class, 81–85; off task student in
geometry class, 125–30; Parents'
Night, 113–21
mnemonics, 72, 74–75
modeling. *See* peer modeling; social
modeling
moral development: academic honesty
case, 17–23; in cyberbullying
case, 25–31; Internet plagiarism
and, 11–15; middle school
biology class and, 21; questions
related to academic honesty
and, 21; questions related to
cyberbullying, adolescent identity
and, 30–31; questions related to
Internet plagiarism and, 14–15;
role of teacher and, 97–106
moral development in adolescence,
questions related to role of
teacher and, 106
mother, student reliance on, 70, 72–73
motivation: academic honesty and,
17–23; academic learning time
and, 125–30; back talk and
disrespect case, 107–12; literature
class and, 110; math anxiety and
lack of student, 81–85; questions
on attributional theory and,
83–84; questions on off-task
student case and, 130; questions
related to middle school academic

STEM (science, technology,
    engineering, and math), 40
stereotypes, gender, 35–43
strategy use, helping students with,
    87–94. *See also* learning
    strategies
stress, high school academic pressure
    and, 87–94
student-centered instruction: authentic
    instruction, funding and, 131–34;
    off task students in middle school
    case study, 125–30; questions
    related to, 129–30
student council, 59
student-directed learning, in high school
    world history portfolios case,
    139–44
students: disinterested, 67–77; engaging
    older high school, 97–106; lack of
    motivation in, 81–85; managing
    off-task, 125–30; teachers as
    friends of, 97–106. *See also* girl
    students
study skills: community service learning
    strategy for improved, 91–92;
    ineffective, 67–77; information
    processing and, 73–74; repetition-
    type tactics, 87

tardiness, 108; teacher allowing, 97
teacher-centered instruction: questions
    related to, 128–29; student-
    centered compared to, 125–30
teacher challenges: academic honesty,
    17–23; academic pressure in
    high school, 87–94; adolescent
    behaviors, 35–43; adolescent
    cliques, 3; adolescent relationships
    and social media influence, 59–65;
    authentic instruction funding, 131,
    132, 136; back talk and disrespect,
    107–12; bullying, 3–9, 25–31,
    57–58; cell phone distractions,
    53–58; cheating, 15, 17–23,
    97–106; choosing appropriate

assessment, 81–85; creating
    authentic learning opportunities,
    131–36; cyberbullying, 25–31;
    defensive or demanding parents,
    67–77; educational technology,
    11–15; engaging disinterested
    students, 67–77; engaging older
    high school students, 97–106;
    gender stereotypes, 35–43; girls'
    confidence in math, 81–85; grade
    complaints, 67–77; grading
    subjective assessment, 139–44;
    helping students with strategy use,
    87–94; identifying and teaching
    students with disabilities, 45–49;
    ineffective study skills, 67–77;
    Internet plagiarism and, 11–15;
    key, ix; lacking instructional
    time, 87–94; linking authentic
    learning with assessment, 131–36;
    managing academic learning
    time, 125–30; managing off-task
    students, 125–30; math anxiety,
    81–85; over-involved parents, 70,
    72–73, 76–77, 88–92, 94; parental
    communications, 81–85, 87–94;
    parental complaints, 87–94;
    peer acceptance, 3–9, 59–65;
    peer rivalry, 17–23; plagiarism,
    11–15, 17–23, 97–106; power
    struggles, 107–12; sexism, 35–43;
    social adjustment, 17–23; social-
    emotional well-being, 25–31;
    social media, 25–31, 53–58,
    59–65, 97–106; social well-being,
    3–9, 59–65; student disruptions,
    81–85; student motivation, 81–85,
    107–12; student stress, 87–94;
    teacher-student interactions,
    97–106; technology use,
    appropriate, 97–106
team teaching, 60
technology: appropriate use of,
    97–106; citing information from
    websites, 13; educational, Internet

About the Authors

Alyssa R. Gonzalez-DeHass received her PhD in educational psychology from the University of Florida in 1998, and she is an associate professor at Florida Atlantic University. She has published in the areas of students' achievement goals, parent involvement, school-community partnerships, and the case study method to teaching educational psychology.

Patricia P. Willems is an associate professor of educational psychology at Florida Atlantic University, where she currently teaches both undergraduate and graduate courses in educational psychology. She earned her PhD in educational psychology from the University of Florida. Her publications are in the areas of case study instruction, learning environments, motivation, school-community partnerships, and parent involvement.

Their coauthored book, *Theories in Educational Psychology: Concise Guide to Meaning and Practice*, was published by Rowman & Littlefield in 2013.

CPSIA information can be obtained
at www.ICGtesting.com
Printed in the USA
BVOW03s2050090917
494410BV00002B/2/P